THE CHATTO BOOK OF
MODERN POETRY

The
Chatto Book
of Modern Poetry
1915–1955

✦ ✦ ✦

Edited by

C. DAY LEWIS
& JOHN LEHMANN

1968

Chatto & Windus
LONDON

Published by
Chatto & Windus Ltd
42 William IV Street
London, W.C. 2

*

Clarke, Irwin & Co. Ltd
Toronto

SBN 7011 0910 6

First Published 1956
New Edition 1959
Reprinted 1966
Reprinted 1968

Printed photolitho in Great Britain
by Ebenezer Baylis and Son, Ltd
The Trinity Press, Worcester, and London

ACKNOWLEDGMENTS

The editors make grateful acknowledgments to the following for permission to use copyright material:—

W. H. Auden and Faber & Faber Ltd. for poems from *Collected Shorter Poems 1930-44*. George Barker and Faber & Faber Ltd. for poems from *A Vision of Beasts and Gods* and *News of the World*. Mr Quentin Bell and The Hogarth Press Ltd. for a poem by Julian Bell from *Julian Bell: Essays, Poems and Letters*, and Chatto & Windus Ltd. for a poem from *Winter Movement*. Frances Bellerby for a poem. John Betjeman and John Murray Ltd. for poems from *A Few Late Chrysanthemums* and *Selected Poems*. Mrs Cicely Binyon and The Society of Authors for poems by Laurence Binyon from *The Burning of the Leaves*. Edmund Blunden for poems from *Poems 1914-1930* (Cobden Sanderson) and *Shells by a Stream* (Macmillan). The Misses Winifred and Muriel Bowes Lyon and Jonathan Cape Ltd. for poems by Lilian Bowes Lyon from *The Collected Poems of Lilian Bowes Lyon*, and the Misses Winifred and Muriel Bowes Lyon for "The Stars Go By". The Clarendon Press, Oxford, for a poem by Robert Bridges from *The Poetical Works of Robert Bridges*. Jocelyn Brooke and John Lane, The Bodley Head Ltd. for a poem from *December Spring*. The author's Executor and J. M. Dent & Sons for poems by Norman Cameron from *The Winter House* and the author's Executor for "A Hook for Leviathan". Roy Campbell and John Lane, The Bodley Head Ltd. for poems from *Collected Poems*. Charles Causley and The Hand & Flower Press for a poem from *Survivor's Leave*. Richard Church and J. M. Dent & Sons for poems from *Collected Poems*. Jack Clemo and Chatto & Windus Ltd. for poems from *The Clay Verge*. Frances Cornford and The Cresset Press Ltd. for a poem from *Collected Poems 1954*. Frances Cornford for a poem by John Cornford. Jonathan Cape Ltd. for poems by W. H. Davies from *The Collected Poems of W. H. Davies*. C. Day Lewis and Jonathan Cape Ltd. and The Hogarth Press Ltd. for poems from *Collected Poems 1954*. Walter de la Mare and Faber & Faber Ltd. for poems from *Collected Poems*. Paul Dehn and Hamish Hamilton Ltd. for a poem from *Romantic Landscape*. Patric Dickinson and Chatto & Windus Ltd. for poems from *The Sailing Race* and *The Scale of Things*. Editions Poetry London for poems by Keith Douglas from *Collected Poems*. Lawrence Durrell and Faber & Faber Ltd. for poems from *A Private Country* and *On Seeming to Presume*. Clifford Dyment and J. M. Dent & Sons Ltd.

v

for poems from *Poems 1935-48* and *Experiences and Places*. T. S. Eliot and Faber & Faber Ltd. for poems from *Collected Poems 1909-1935* and for "East Coker". William Empson and Chatto & Windus Ltd. for poems from *Collected Poems*. G. S. Fraser and the Harvill Press for a poem from *The Traveller Has Regrets*. Mrs Freeman for a poem by John Freeman. Roy Fuller and Derek Verschoyle Ltd. for poems from *Counterparts* and The Hogarth Press Ltd. for poems from *A Lost Season*. David Gascoyne and John Lehmann Ltd. for a poem from *A Vagrant*: David Gascoyne and Editions Poetry London for poems from *Poems 1937-42*. W. S. Graham and Faber & Faber Ltd. for a poem from *The Night-Fishing*. Robert Graves for poems from *Collected Poems (1914-1947)* (Cassell). J. C. Hall for a poem from *The Summer Dance* (John Lehmann Ltd.). The Trustees of the Hardy Estate and Macmillan & Co. Ltd. for poems by Thomas Hardy from *Collected Poems*. John Heath-Stubbs and Methuen & Co. Ltd. for a poem from *A Charm Against the Toothache*. Hamish Henderson and John Lehmann Ltd. for a poem from *Elegies for the Dead in Cyrenaica*. Rayner Heppenstall and Secker & Warburg Ltd. for a poem from *Blind Men's Flowers Are Green*. The Society of Authors as the literary Representative of the Trustees of the Estate of the late A. E. Housman, and Jonathan Cape Ltd., for poems by A. E. Housman from *Collected Poems*. Mrs George Bambridge and Methuen & Co. Ltd. for a poem by Rudyard Kipling from *The Years Between*; Macmillan & Co. Ltd. for a poem from *A Diversity of Creatures* and a poem from *The Definitive Edition of Rudyard Kipling's Verse* (Hodder & Stoughton). The author's Executors and Routledge & Kegan Paul Ltd. for poems by Sidney Keyes from *Collected Poems*. James Kirkup and Oxford University Press for "A Correct Compassion". Mrs Frieda Lawrence and William Heinemann Ltd. for poems by D. H. Lawrence from *Collected Poems*. Laurie Lee and The Hogarth Press Ltd. for poems from *The Sun My Monument* and John Lehmann Ltd. for a poem from *A Bloom of Candles*. John Lehmann and Longmans, Green & Co. Ltd. for poems from *The Age of the Dragon*. Alun Lewis and George Allen & Unwin Ltd. for poems from *Ha! Ha! Among the Trumpets*. John Masefield and the Society of Authors for poems from *Collected Poems* and *A Letter from Pontus*. Mrs Harold Monro and Gerald Duckworth & Co. Ltd. for poems by Charlotte Mew from *Collected Poems*. Mrs Monro for a poem by Harold Monro from *Midnight Lamentation*. Edwin Muir and Faber & Faber Ltd. for poems from *Collected Poems 1921-51* and *One Foot in Eden*. Louis MacNeice and Faber & Faber Ltd. for poems from *Collected Poems 1925-48*. The author's literary Executor and William Collins & Co. Ltd. for poems by Robert

ACKNOWLEDGMENTS

Nichols from *Such Was My Singing*. Norman Nicholson and Faber & Faber Ltd. for poems from *Five Rivers, Rock Face* and *The Pot Geranium*. Miss Mary Owen and Chatto & Windus Ltd. for poems by Wilfred Owen from *Poems*. Ruth Pitter and The Cresset Press Ltd. for a poem from *Urania*. William Plomer and Jonathan Cape Ltd. for poems from *Visiting the Caves* and The Hogarth Press Ltd. for a poem from *Selected Poems*. F. T. Prince and the Fortune Press for poems from *Soldiers Bathing and Other Poems*. Peter Quennell and Chatto & Windus Ltd. for poems from *Poems*. Kathleen Raine and Hamish Hamilton Ltd. for poems from *The Pythoness* and *The Year One*; and Editions Poetry London for a poem from *Stone and Flower*. Herbert Read and Faber & Faber Ltd. for poems from *Collected Poems*. Henry Reed and Jonathan Cape Ltd. for poems from *A Map of Verona*. James Reeves and William Heinemann Ltd. for a poem from *The Password and Other Poems*. Edgell Rickword and John Lane, The Bodley Head Ltd. for poems from *Collected Poems*. Anne Ridler and Faber & Faber Ltd. for poems from *The Nine Bright Shiners* and *The Golden Bird*. Lynette Roberts for a poem. Faber & Faber Ltd. for poems by Michael Roberts from *Orion Marches*. W. R. Rodgers and Secker & Warburg Ltd. for poems from *Awake* and *Europa and the Bull*. Mrs A. Wynick and Chatto & Windus Ltd. for poems by Isaac Rosenberg from *The Collected Poems of Isaac Rosenberg*. Alan Ross and Derek Verschoyle Ltd. for a poem from *Something of the Sea*. V. Sackville-West and The Hogarth Press Ltd. for poems from *Collected Poems*. Siegfried Sassoon and Faber & Faber Ltd. for poems from *Collected Poems*. E. J. Scovell and The Cresset Press Ltd. for poems from The River Steamer and *Shadows of Chrysanthemums*. Mrs E. Maitland and Miss M. Fisher and The Hogarth Press Ltd. for poems by Fredegond Shove. Edith Sitwell and Macmillan & Co. Ltd. for poems from *Canticle of the Rose* and *Gardeners and Astronomers*. Osbert Sitwell and Gerald Duckworth & Co. Ltd. for poems from *Selected Poems—Old and New*. Sacheverell Sitwell and Gerald Duckworth & Co. Ltd. for poems from *Selected Poems*. Stanley Snaith and Jonathan Cape Ltd. for poems from *Green Legacy*. Bernard Spencer and Editions Poetry London for poems from *Aegean Islands*. Stephen Spender and Faber & Faber Ltd. for poems from *Collected Poems*. Helen Spalding and Methuen & Co. Ltd. for a poem from *What Images Return*. Hal Summers and J. M. Dent & Sons for poems from *Hinterland and Other Poems*. A. S. J. Tessimond for poems from *The Walls of Glass* (Methuen) and a poem from *Voices in a Giant City* (Heinemann). The Trustees of the author's Estate and J. M. Dent & Sons for poems by Dylan Thomas from *Collected Poems 1934-52*. Mrs Helen Thomas

ACKNOWLEDGMENTS

and Faber & Faber Ltd. for poems by Edward Thomas from *Collected Poems*. R. S. Thomas and Rupert Hart-Davis Ltd. for poems from *Song at the Year's Turning*. Terence Tiller and The Hogarth Press Ltd. for poems from *Unarm Eros* and *The Inward Animal*. Oxford University Press for a poem by W. J. Turner from *Poems*. Rex Warner and John Lane, The Bodley Head Ltd. for a poem from *Poems and Contradictions*. Vernon Watkins and Faber & Faber Ltd. for poems from *Ballad of the Mari Lwyd*, *The Lady with the Unicorn* and *The Death Bell*; also the Editor of *The London Magazine* for one poem. Dorothy Wellesley for a poem from *Selected Poems* (Williams & Norgate Ltd.). Sheila Wingfield and The Cresset Press Ltd. for a poem from *A Kite's Dinner*. Diana Witherby and Derek Verschoyle Ltd. for a poem from *Poems*. David Wright and Derek Verschoyle Ltd. for a poem from *Moral Stories*. Peter Yates and Chatto & Windus Ltd. for poems from *Dark and Light* and *The Motionless Dancer*. Mrs Yeats and Macmillan & Co. Ltd. for poems by W. B. Yeats from *Collected Poems of W. B. Yeats*. Andrew Young and Jonathan Cape Ltd. for poems from *Collected Poems of Andrew Young*. Norman MacCaig and The Hogarth Press Ltd. for a poem from *Riding Lights*.

INTRODUCTION

IN making our choice from the poetry of the last forty years, our guiding principle has been to show its range and variety, while at the same time weighting the selection in favour of the poets of outstanding achievement and influence. A number of interesting poets who flourished during the earlier years of the period are thinly represented, or not at all: we think they have had their due in previous anthologies. Again, we have excluded writers who, when we made our final selection, had not reached the age of thirty: more time is needed before we can see the verse of the youngest generation in perspective, or judge its merits fairly. We have also excluded American and other English-speaking poets from overseas, poetry written in dialect, and translations—even those, such as Dr Waley's, which have almost the status of original poems.

All such limitations have an arbitrary look; but physical limits there must be to any anthology. We took 1915 as a starting date because the earlier years of the First World War produced an obvious change of temper in English poetry—dividing Rupert Brooke, for instance, from Wilfred Owen. What an anthology finally represents, however "representative" it may claim to be, is the taste and interests of its editors at the time of its making. If this one brings to light for each reader some poets he had not known, and sends him back with renewed sympathy to the work of others, it will have served its purpose.

C. DAY LEWIS

JOHN LEHMANN

CONTENTS

3

4

THOMAS HARDY

The Haunter

He does not think that I haunt here nightly:
   How shall I let him know
That whither his fancy sets him wandering
   I, too, alertly go?—
Hover and hover a few feet from him
   Just as I used to do,
But cannot answer the words he lifts me—
   Only listen thereto!

When I could answer he did not say them:
   When I could let him know
How I would like to join in his journeys
   Seldom he wished to go.
Now that he goes and wants me with him
   More than he used to do,
Never he sees my faithful phantom
   Though he speaks thereto.

Yes, I companion him to places
   Only dreamers know,
Where the shy hares print long paces,
   Where the night rooks go;
Into old aisles where the past is all to him,
   Close as his shade can do,
Always lacking the power to call to him,
   Near as I reach thereto!

What a good haunter I am, O tell him!
   Quickly make him know
If he but sigh since my loss befell him
   Straight to his side I go.
Tell him a faithful one is doing
   All that love can do
Still that his path may be worth pursuing,
   And to bring peace thereto.

13

THOMAS HARDY

After a Journey

Hereto I come to view a voiceless ghost;
   Whither, O whither will its whim now draw me?
Up the cliff, down, till I'm lonely, lost,
   And the unseen waters' ejaculations awe me.
Where you will next be there's no knowing,
    Facing round about me everywhere,
      With your nut-coloured hair,
And grey eyes, and rose-flush coming and going.

Yes: I have re-entered your olden haunts at last;
   Through the years, through the dead scenes I have tracked you;
What have you now found to say of our past—
   Scanned across the dark space wherein I have lacked you?
Summer gave us sweets, but autumn wrought division?
    Things were not lastly as firstly well
      With us twain, you tell?
But all's closed now, despite Time's derision.

I see what you are doing: you are leading me on
   To the spots we knew when we haunted here together,
The waterfall, above which the mist-bow shone
   At the then fair hour in the then fair weather,
And the cave just under, with a voice still so hollow
    That it seems to call out to me from forty years ago,
      When you were all aglow,
And not the thin ghost that I now frailly follow!

Ignorant of what there is flitting here to see,
   The waked birds preen and the seals flop lazily;
Soon you will have, Dear, to vanish from me,
   For the stars close their shutters and the dawn whitens hazily.
Trust me, I mind not, though Life lours,
    The bringing me here; nay, bring me here again!
      I am just the same as when
Our days were a joy, and our paths through flowers.

THOMAS HARDY

At Lulworth Cove a Century Back

Had I but lived a hundred years ago
I might have gone, as I have gone this year,
By Warmwell Cross on to a Cove I know,
And Time have placed his finger on me there:

"*You see that man?*"—I might have looked, and said,
"O yes: I see him. One that boat has brought
Which dropped down Channel round Saint Alban's Head.
So commonplace a youth calls not my thought."

"*You see that man?*"—"Why yes; I told you; yes:
Of an idling town-sort; thin; hair brown in hue;
And as the evening light scants less and less
He looks up at a star, as many do."

"*You see that man?*"—"Nay, leave me!" then I plead,
"I have fifteen miles to vamp across the lea,
And it grows dark, and I am weary-kneed:
I have said the third time; yes, that man I see!"

"Good. That man goes to Rome—to death, despair;
And no one notes him now but you and I:
A hundred years, and the world will follow him there,
And bend with reverence where his ashes lie."

September 1920.

NOTE. In September 1820 Keats, on his way to Rome, landed one
day on the Dorset coast, and composed the sonnet, "Bright star! would
I were steadfast as thou art." The spot of his landing is judged to have
been Lulworth Cove.

THOMAS HARDY

Afterwards

When the Present has latched its postern behind my tremulous stay,
    And the May month flaps its glad green leaves like wings,
Delicate-filmed as new-spun silk, will the neighbours say,
    "He was a man who used to notice such things"?

If it be in the dusk when, like an eyelid's soundless blink,
    The dewfall-hawk comes crossing the shades to alight,
Upon the wind-warped upland thorn, a gazer may think,
    "To him this must have been a familiar sight."

If I pass during some nocturnal blackness, mothy and warm,
    When the hedgehog travels furtively over the lawn,
One may say, "He strove that such innocent creatures should
      come to no harm,
    But he could do little for them; and now he is gone."

If, when hearing that I have been stilled at last, they stand at
      the door,
    Watching the full-starred heavens that winter sees,
Will this thought rise on those who will meet my face no more,
    "He was one who had an eye for such mysteries"?

And will any say when my bell of quittance is heard in the gloom,
    And a crossing breeze cuts a pause in its outrollings,
Till they rise again, as they were a new bell's boom,
    "He hears it not now, but used to notice such things"?

An Ancient to Ancients

Where once we danced, where once we sang,
        Gentlemen,
The floors are sunken, cobwebs hang,
And cracks creep; worms have fed upon
The doors. Yea, sprightlier times were then
Than now, with harps and tabrets gone,
        Gentlemen!

Where once we rowed, where once we sailed
    Gentlemen,
And damsels took the tiller, veiled
Against too strong a stare (God wot
Their fancy, then or anywhen!)
Upon that shore we are clean forgot,
    Gentlemen!

We have lost somewhat, afar and near,
    Gentlemen,
The thinning of our ranks each year ·
Affords a hint we are nigh undone,
That we shall not be ever again
The marked of many, loved of one,
    Gentlemen.

In dance the polka hit our wish,
    Gentlemen,
The paced quadrille, the spry schottische,
"Sir Roger."—And in opera spheres
The "Girl" (the famed "Bohemian"),
And "Trovatore," held the ears,
    Gentlemen.

This season's paintings do not please,
    Gentlemen,
Like Etty, Mulready, Maclise;
Throbbing romance has waned and wanned;
No wizard wields the witching pen
Of Bulwer, Scott, Dumas, and Sand,
    Gentlemen.

The bower we shrined to Tennyson,
    Gentlemen,
Is roof-wrecked; damps there drip upon
Sagged seats, the creeper-nails are rust,
The spider is sole denizen;
Even she who voiced those rhymes is dust,
    Gentlemen!

THOMAS HARDY

We who met sunrise sanguine-souled,
    Gentlemen,
Are wearing weary. We are old;
These younger press; we feel our rout
Is imminent to Aïdes' den,—
That evening shades are stretching out,
    Gentlemen!

And yet, though ours be failing frames,
    Gentlemen,
So were some others' history names,
Who trode their track light-limbed and fast
As these youth, and not alien
From enterprise, to their long last,
    Gentlemen.

Sophocles, Plato, Socrates,
    Gentlemen,
Pythagoras, Thucydides,
Herodotus, and Homer,—yea,
Clement, Augustin, Origen,
Burnt brightlier towards their setting-day,
    Gentlemen.

And ye, red-lipped and smooth-browed; list,
    Gentlemen;
Much is there waits you we have missed;
Much lore we leave you worth the knowing,
Much, much has lain outside our ken:
Nay, rush not: time serves: we are going,
    Gentlemen.

THOMAS HARDY

Surview

"Cogitavi vias meas"

A cry from the green-grained sticks of the fire
  Made me gaze where it seemed to be:
'Twas my own voice talking therefrom to me
On how I had walked when my sun was higher—
  My heart in its arrogancy.

"You held not to whatsoever was true,"
  Said my own voice talking to me:
*"Whatsoever was just you were slack to see;
Kept not things lovely and pure in view,"*
  Said my own voice talking to me.

"You slighted her that endureth all,"
  Said my own voice talking to me;
*"Vaunteth not, trusteth hopefully;
That suffereth long and is kind withal,"*
  Said my own voice talking to me.

"You taught not that which you set about,"
  Said my own voice talking to me;
"That the greatest of things is Charity. . . ."
—And the sticks burnt low, and the fire went out,
  And my voice ceased talking to me.

ROBERT BRIDGES

Cheddar Pinks

Mid the squander'd colour
  idling as I lay
Reading the Odyssey
  in my rock-garden
I espied the cluster'd
  tufts of Cheddar pinks

Burgeoning with promise
   of their scented bloom
All the modish motley
   of their bloom to-be
Thrust up in narrow buds
   on the slender stalks
Thronging springing urgent
   hasting (so I thought)
As if they feared to be
   too late for summer—
Like schoolgirls overslept
   waken'd by the bell
Leaping from bed to don
   their muslin dresses
     On a May morning:

Then felt I like to one
   indulging in sin
(Whereto Nature is oft
   a blind accomplice)
Because my aged bones
   so enjoyed the sun
There as I lay along
   idling with my thoughts
Reading an old poet
   while the busy world
Toil'd moil'd fuss'd and scurried
   worried bought and sold
Plotted stole and quarrelled
   fought and God knows what.
I had forgotten Homer
   dallying with my thoughts
Till I fell to making
   these little verses
Communing with the flowers
   in my rock-garden
     On a May morning.

A. E. HOUSMAN

Tell me Not Here

Tell me not here, it needs not saying,
    What tune the enchantress plays
In aftermaths of soft September
    Or under blanching mays,
For she and I were long acquainted
    And I knew all her ways.

On russet floors, by waters idle,
    The pine lets fall its cone;
The cuckoo shouts all day at nothing
    In leafy dells alone;
And traveller's joy beguiles in autumn
    Hearts that have lost their own.

On acres of the seeded grasses
    The changing burnish heaves;
Or marshalled under moons of harvest
    Stand still all night the sheaves;
Or beeches strip in storms for winter
    And stain the wind with leaves.

Possess, as I possessed a season,
    The countries I resign,
Where over elmy plains the highway
    Would mount the hills and shine,
And full of shade the pillared forest
    Would murmur and be mine.

For nature, heartless, witless nature,
    Will neither care nor know
What stranger's feet may find the meadow
    And trespass there and go,
Nor ask amid the dews of morning
    If they are mine or no.

A. E. HOUSMAN

Crossing Alone the Nighted Ferry

Crossing alone the nighted ferry
  With the one coin for fee,
Whom, on the wharf of Lethe waiting,
  Count you to find? Not me.

The brisk fond lackey to fetch and carry,
  The true, sick-hearted slave,
Expect him not in the just city
  And free land of the grave.

Easter Hymn

If in that Syrian garden, ages slain,
You sleep, and know not you are dead in vain,
Nor even in dreams behold how dark and bright
Ascends in smoke and fire by day and night
The hate you died to quench and could but fan,
Sleep well and see no morning, son of man.

But if, the grave rent and the stone rolled by,
At the right hand of majesty on high
You sit, and sitting so remember yet
Your tears, your agony and bloody sweat,
Your cross and passion, and the life you gave,
Bow hither out of heaven and see and save.

Oh Who is that Young Sinner?

Oh who is that young sinner with the handcuffs on his wrists?
And what has he been after that they groan and shake their fists?
And wherefore is he wearing such a conscience-stricken air?
Oh they're taking him to prison for the colour of his hair.

A. E. HOUSMAN

'Tis a shame to human nature, such a head of hair as his;
In the good old time 'twas hanging for the colour that it is;
Though hanging isn't bad enough and flaying would be fair
For the nameless and abominable colour of his hair.

Oh a deal of pains he's taken and a pretty price he's paid
To hide his poll or dye it of a mentionable shade;
But they've pulled the beggar's hat off for the world to see and stare,
And they're taking him to justice for the colour of his hair.

Now 'tis oakum for his fingers and the treadmill for his feet,
And the quarry-gang of Portland in the cold and in the heat,
And between his spells of labour in the time he has to spare
He can curse the God that made him for the colour of his hair.

RUDYARD KIPLING

The Fabulists

1914-1918

When all the world would keep a matter hid,
  Since Truth is seldom friend to any crowd,
Men write in fable as old Æsop did,
  Jesting at that which none will name aloud.
And this they needs must do, or it will fall
Unless they please they are not heard at all.

When desperate Folly daily laboureth
  To work confusion upon all we have,
When diligent Sloth demandeth Freedom's death,
  And banded Fear commandeth Honour's grave—
Even in that certain hour before the fall,
Unless men please they are not heard at all.

Needs must all please, yet some not all for need,
  Needs must all toil, yet some not all for gain,
But that men taking pleasure may take heed,
  Whom present toil shall snatch from later pain.
Thus some have toiled, but their reward was small
Since, though they pleased, they were not heard at all.

This was the lock that lay upon our lips,
　　This was the yoke that we have undergone,
Denying us all pleasant fellowships
　　As in our time and generation
Our pleasures unpursued age past recall,
And for our pains—we are not heard at all.

What man hears aught except the groaning guns?
　　What man heeds aught save what each instant brings
When each man's life all imaged life outruns,
　　What man shall pleasure in imaginings?
So it has fallen, as it was bound to fall,
We are not, nor we were not, heard at all.

The Storm Cone

1932

　　This is the midnight—let no star
　　Delude us—dawn is very far.
　　This is the tempest long foretold—
　　Slow to make head but sure to hold.

　　Stand by! The lull 'twixt blast and blast
　　Signals the storm is near, not past;
　　And worse than present jeopardy
　　May our forlorn tomorrow be.

　　If we have cleared the expectant reef,
　　Let no man look for his relief.
　　Only the darkness hides the shape
　　Of further peril to escape.

　　It is decreed that we abide
　　The weight of gale against the tide
　　And those huge waves the outer main
　　Sends in to set us back again.

They fall and whelm. We strain to hear
The pulses of her labouring gear,
Till the deep throb beneath us proves,
After each shudder and check she moves!

She moves, with all save purpose lost,
To make her offing from the coast;
But, till she fetches open sea,
Let no man deem that he is free!

A Son

My son was killed while laughing at some jest. I would I knew
What it was, and it might serve me in a time when jests are few.

W. B. YEATS

Easter 1916

I have met them at close of day
Coming with vivid faces
From counter or desk among grey
Eighteenth-century houses.
I have passed with a nod of the head
Or polite meaningless words,
Or have lingered awhile and said
Polite meaningless words,
And thought before I had done
Of a mocking tale or a gibe
To please a companion
Around the fire at the club,
Being certain that they and I
But lived where motley is worn:
All changed, changed utterly:
A terrible beauty is born.

That woman's days were spent
In ignorant good-will,
Her nights in argument
Until her voice grew shrill.
What voice more sweet than hers
When, young and beautiful,
She rode to harriers?
This man had kept a school
And rode our wingèd horse;
This other his helper and friend
Was coming into his force;
He might have won fame in the end,
So sensitive his nature seemed,
So daring and sweet his thought.
This other man I had dreamed
A drunken vainglorious lout.
He had done most bitter wrong
To some who are near my heart,
Yet I number him in the song;
He, too, has resigned his part
In the casual comedy;
He, too, has been changed in his turn,
Transformed utterly:
A terrible beauty is born.

Hearts with one purpose alone
Through summer and winter seem
Enchanted to a stone
To trouble the living stream
The horse that comes from the road,
The rider, the birds that range
From cloud to tumbling cloud,
Minute by minute they change;
A shadow of cloud on the stream
Changes minute by minute;
A horse-hoof slides on the brim,
And a horse plashes within it;

The long-legged moor-hens dive,
And hens to moor-cocks call;
Minute by minute they live:
The stone's in the midst of all.

Too long a sacrifice
Can make a stone of the heart.
O when may it suffice?
That is Heaven's part, our part
To murmur name upon name,
As a mother names her child
When sleep at last has come
On limbs that had run wild.
What is it but nightfall?
No, no, not night but death;
Was it needless death after all?
For England may keep faith
For all that is done and said.
We know their dream; enough
To know they dreamed and are dead;
And what if excess of love
Bewildered them till they died?
I write it out in a verse—
MacDonagh and MacBride
And Connolly and Pearse
Now and in time to be,
Wherever green is worn,
Are changed, changed utterly:
A terrible beauty is born.

Leda and the Swan

A sudden blow: the great wings beating still
Above the staggering girl, her thighs caressed
By the dark webs, her nape caught in his bill,
He holds her helpless breast upon his breast.

How can those terrified vague fingers push
The feathered glory from her loosening thighs?
And how can body, laid in that white rush,
But feel the strange heart beating where it lies?

A shudder in the loins engenders there
The broken wall, the burning roof and tower
And Agamemnon dead.
                  Being so caught up,
So mastered by the brute blood of the air,
Did she put on his knowledge with his power
Before the indifferent beak could let her drop?

Sailing to Byzantium

I

That is no country for old men. The young
In one another's arms, birds in the trees
—Those dying generations—at their song,
The salmon-falls, the mackerel-crowded seas,
Fish, flesh, or fowl, commend all summer long
Whatever is begotten, born and dies.
Caught in that sensual music all neglect
Monuments of unageing intellect.

II

An aged man is but a paltry thing,
A tattered coat upon a stick, unless
Soul clap its hands and sing, and louder sing
For every tatter in its mortal dress,
Nor is there singing school but studying
Monuments of its own magnificence;
And therefore I have sailed the seas and come
To the holy city of Byzantium.

III

O sages standing in God's holy fire
As in the gold mosaic of a wall,
Come from the holy fire, perne in a gyre,
And be the singing-masters of my soul.
Consume my heart away; sick with desire
And fastened to a dying animal
It knows not what it is; and gather me
Into the artifice of eternity.

IV

Once out of nature I shall never take
My bodily form from any natural thing,
But such a form as Grecian goldsmiths make
Of hammered gold and gold enamelling
To keep a drowsy Emperor awake;
Or set upon a golden bough to sing
To lords and ladies of Byzantium
Of what is past, or passing, or to come.

Ancestral Houses

Surely among a rich man's flowering lawns,
Amid the rustle of his planted hills,
Life overflows without ambitious pains;
And rains down life until the basin spills,
And mounts more dizzy high the more it rains
As though to choose whatever shape it wills
And never stoop to a mechanical
Or servile shape, at others' beck and call.

Mere dreams, mere dreams! Yet Homer had not sung
Had he not found it certain beyond dreams
That out of life's own self-delight had sprung
The abounding glittering jet; though now it seems

As if some marvellous empty sea-shell flung
Out of the obscure dark of the rich streams,
And not a fountain, were the symbol which
Shadows the inherited glory of the rich.

Some violent bitter man, some powerful man
Called architect and artist in, that they,
Bitter and violent men, might rear in stone
The sweetness that all longed for night and day,
The gentleness none there had ever known;
But when the master's buried mice can play,
And maybe the great-grandson of that house,
For all its bronze and marble, 's but a mouse.

O what if gardens where the peacock strays
With delicate feet upon old terraces,
Or else all Juno from an urn displays
Before the indifferent garden deities;
O what if levelled lawns and gravelled ways
Where slippered Contemplation finds his ease
And Childhood a delight for every sense,
But take our greatness with our violence?

What if the glory of escutcheoned doors,
And buildings that a haughtier age designed,
The pacing to and fro on polished floors
Amid great chambers and long galleries, lined
With famous portraits of our ancestors;
What if those things the greatest of mankind
Consider most to magnify, or to bless,
But take our greatness with our bitterness?

Among School Children

I

I walk through the long schoolroom questioning;
A kind old nun in a white hood replies;
The children learn to cipher and to sing,
To study reading-books and histories,

To cut and sew, be neat in everything
In the best modern way—the children's eyes
In momentary wonder stare upon
A sixty-year-old smiling public man.

II

I dream of a Ledaean body, bent
Above a sinking fire, a tale that she
Told of a harsh reproof, or trivial event
That changed some childish day to tragedy—
Told, and it seemed that our two natures blent
Into a sphere from youthful sympathy,
Or else, to alter Plato's parable,
Into the yolk and white of the one shell.

III

And thinking of that fit of grief or rage
I look upon one child or t'other there
And wonder if she stood so at that age—
For even daughters of the swan can share
Something of every paddler's heritage—
And had that colour upon cheek, or hair,
And thereupon my heart is driven wild:
She stands before me as a living child.

IV

Her present image floats into the mind—
Did Quattrocento finger fashion it
Hollow of cheek as though it drank the wind
And took a mess of shadows for its meat?
And I though never of Ledaean kind
Had pretty plumage once—enough of that,
Better to smile on all that smile, and show
There is a comfortable kind of old scarecrow.

V

What youthful mother, a shape upon her lap
Honey of generation had betrayed,
And that must sleep, shriek, struggle to escape
As recollection or the drug decide,
Would think her son, did she but see that shape
With sixty or more winters on its head,
A compensation for the pang of his birth,
Or the uncertainty of his setting forth?

VI

Plato thought nature but a spume that plays
Upon a ghostly paradigm of things;
Solider Aristotle played the taws
Upon the bottom of a king of kings;
World-famous golden-thighed Pythagoras
Fingered upon a fiddle-stick or strings
What a star sang and careless Muses heard:
Old clothes upon old sticks to scare a bird.

VII

Both nuns and mothers worship images,
But those the candles light are not as those
That animate a mother's reveries,
But keep a marble or a bronze repose.
And yet they too break hearts—O Presences
That passion, piety or affection knows,
And that all heavenly glory symbolise—
O self-born mockers of man's enterprise;

VIII

Labour is blossoming or dancing where
The body is not bruised to pleasure soul,
Nor beauty born out of its own despair,
Nor blear-eyed wisdom out of midnight oil.

O chestnut tree, great-rooted blossomer,
Are you the leaf, the blossom or the bole?
O body swayed to music, O brightening glance,
How can we know the dancer from the dance?

Death

Nor dread nor hope attend
A dying animal;
A man awaits his end
Dreading and hoping all;
Many times he died,
Many times rose again.
A great man in his pride
Confronting murderous men
Casts derision upon
Supersession of breath;
He knows death to the bone—
Man has created death.

Lapis Lazuli

For Harry Clifton

I have heard that hysterical women say
They are sick of the palette and fiddle-bow,
Of poets that are always gay,
For everybody knows or else should know
That if nothing drastic is done
Aeroplane and Zeppelin will come out,
Pitch like King Billy bomb-balls in
Until the town lie beaten flat.

All perform their tragic play,
There struts Hamlet, there is Lear,
That's Ophelia, that Cordelia;
Yet they, should the last scene be there,

The great stage curtain about to drop,
If worthy their prominent part in the play,
Do not break up their lines to weep.
They know that Hamlet and Lear are gay;
Gaiety transfiguring all that dread.
All men have aimed at, found and lost;
Black out; Heaven blazing into the head:
Tragedy wrought to its uttermost.
Though Hamlet rambles and Lear rages,
And all the drop-scenes drop at once
Upon a hundred thousand stages,
It cannot grow by an inch or an ounce.

On their own feet they came, or on shipboard,
Camel-back, horse-back, ass-back, mule-back,
Old civilisations put to the sword.
Then they and their wisdom went to rack:
No handiwork of Callimachus,
Who handled marble as if it were bronze,
Made draperies that seemed to rise
When sea-winds swept the corner, stands;
His long lamp-chimney shaped like the stem
Of a slender palm, stood but a day;
All things fall and are built again,
And those that build them again are gay.

Two Chinamen, behind them a third,
Are carved in lapis lazuli,
Over them flies a long-legged bird,
A symbol of longevity;
The third, doubtless a serving-man,
Carries a musical instrument.

Every discoloration of the stone,
Every accidental crack or dent,
Seems a water-course or an avalanche,
Or lofty slope where it still snows

Though doubtless plum or cherry-branch
Sweetens the little half-way house
Those Chinamen climb towards, and I
Delight to imagine them seated there;
There, on the mountain and the sky,
On all the tragic scene they stare.
One asks for mournful melodies;
Accomplished fingers begin to play.
Their eyes mid many wrinkles, their eyes,
Their ancient, glittering eyes, are gay.

LAURENCE BINYON

The Burning of the Leaves

Now is the time for the burning of the leaves.
They go to the fire; the nostril pricks with smoke
Wandering slowly into a weeping mist.
Brittle and blotched, ragged and rotten sheaves!
A flame seizes the smouldering ruin and bites
On stubborn stalks that crackle as they resist.

The last hollyhock's fallen tower is dust;
All the spices of June are a bitter reek,
All the extravagant riches spent and mean.
All burns! The reddest rose is a ghost;
Sparks whirl up, to expire in the mist: the wild
Fingers of fire are making corruption clean.

Now is the time for stripping the spirit bare,
Time for the burning of days ended and done,
Idle solace of things that have gone before:
Rootless hope and fruitless desire are there;
Let them go to the fire, with never a look behind.
The world that was ours is a world that is ours no more.

They will come again, the leaf and the flower, to arise
From squalor of rottenness into the old splendour,
And magical scents to a wondering memory bring;
The same glory, to shine upon different eyes.
Earth cares for her own ruins, naught for ours.
Nothing is certain, only the certain spring.

Ezekiel

Ezekiel in the valley of Dry Bones
Heard the word of the Lord commanding him:
"Prophesy to these bones that they may live."
There was a noise and a shaking; and bone to bone
Clove together, and sinew and flesh came on them.

Yet there was no breath in them. The Lord commanded:
"Prophesy, Son of Man, to the four winds."
And the winds came from the corners of the earth,
Breathing upon those dead, and clothed in flesh
Was a great army standing upon their feet.

I dreamed I stood in a valley of dry bones.
But what were these? derelict, rusty, mounded
Clutter and offal of man's invention, dry bones
Cast aside by hurrying civilization,
Yesterday's triumph, that To-day despises.

With a noise of hissing they were coming together.
Fire breathed on them, and metal clove to metal,
Timed and measured, each to its intricate function,
Minute or monstrous, all in the brain engendered,
Convolutions, multiplied over and over.

Panting and humming, forms combined to a meaning,
Usurping the sky, supplanting the sweet verdure,
Forms from the blinding furnace issuing, huge
Giantry of metal, dwarfing man to a pigmy,
Sounding, clamouring, throbbing in speed and power.

36

LAURENCE BINYON

Proud we gaze on all we have mastered,—captive
Force, and willed conformity, stamped exactness.
But O divine diversity of creatures,
Where are you? Not here amid man's contrivings;
None can repeat you, none complete, nor annul you.

from *Winter Sunrise*

It is early morning within this room; without,
Dark and damp; without and within, stillness
Waiting for day: not a sound but a listening air.

Yellow jasmine, delicate on stiff branches
Stands in a Tuscan pot to delight the eye
In spare December's patient nakedness.

Suddenly, softly, as if a breath breathed
On the pale wall, a magical apparition,
The shadow of the jasmine, branch and blossom!

It was not there, it is there, in a perfect image;
And all is changed. It is like a memory lost
Returning without a reason into the mind:

And it seems to me that the beauty of the shadow
Is more beautiful than the flower; a strange beauty,
Pencilled and silently deepening to distinctness.

As a memory stealing out of the mind's slumber,
A memory floating up from a dark water,
Can be more beautiful than the thing remembered.

CHARLOTTE MEW

The Call

From our low seat beside the fire
   Where we have dozed and dreamed and watched
     the glow
Or raked the ashes, stopping so
We scarcely saw the sun or rain
   Above, or looked much higher
Than this same quiet red or burned-out fire,
        To-night we heard a call,
        A rattle on the window-pane,
        A voice on the sharp air,
And felt a breath stirring our hair,
   A flame within us: Something swift and tall
   Swept in and out and that was all.
Was it a bright or a dark angel? Who can know?
   It left no mark upon the snow,
     But suddenly it snapped the chain,
     Unbarred, flung wide the door
     Which will not shut again;
   And so we cannot sit here any more.
        We must arise and go:
     The world is cold without
     And dark and hedged about
   With mystery and enmity and doubt,
     But we must go
     Though yet we do not know
Who called, or what marks we shall leave upon the snow.

Absence

Sometimes I know the way
   You walk, up over the bay;
It is a wind from that far sea
That blows the fragrance of your hair to me.

Or in this garden when the breeze
   Touches my trees
To stir their dreaming shadows on the grass
   I see you pass.

In sheltered beds, the heart of every rose
   Serenely sleeps tonight. As shut as those
Your guarded heart; as safe as they from the beat, beat
Of hooves that tread dropped roses in the street.

   Turn never again
   On these eyes blind with a wild rain
Your eyes; they were stars to me.—
   There are things stars may not see.

But call, call, and though Christ stands
   Still with scarred hands
Over my mouth, I must answer. So,
I will come—He shall let me go!

Moorland Night

My face is against the grass—the moorland grass is wet—
   My eyes are shut against the grass, against my lips there are
      the little blades,
   Over my head the curlews call,
  And now there is the night wind in my hair;
My heart is against the grass and the sweet earth;—it has gone
still, at last.
   It does not want to beat any more,
     And why should it beat?
   This is the end of the journey;
     The Thing is found.

   This is the end of all the roads—
  Over the grass there is the night-dew
And the wind that drives up from the sea along the moorland
road;

I hear a curlew start out from the heath
And fly off, calling through the dusk,
   The wild, long, rippling call.
The Thing is found and I am quiet with the earth.
Perhaps the earth will hold it, or the wind, or that bird's cry,
But it is not for long in any life I know. This cannot stay,
Not now, not yet, not in a dying world, with me, for very long.
   I leave it here:
   And one day the wet grass may give it back—
   One day the quiet earth may give it back—
   The calling birds may give it back as they go by—
To someone walking on the moor who starves for love and will not
   Who gave it to all these to give away;   know
   Or, if I come and ask for it again,
   Oh! then, to me.

W. H. DAVIES

An Epitaph

Beneath this stone lies one good man; and when
We say his kindly thought towards all men
Was as generous to the living as to the dead—
What more for any mortal could be said?
His only enemies were those he tried
To help, and failed; who blamed him, in their pride,
Forgetting that his power was not as great
As his intention—and their own weak state.
And if he met with men too slow to move
Into the fullness of his own clear love,
He looked for the fault in his own self, and not
Blamed other men—like our more common lot.
His boundless trust and innocence of evil
Tempted the base and mean, and helped the devil.
Since such a man, without suspicion, kind,
Was duped by many a false, ungrateful mind,
He's gone to Heaven—because he lived so well
That many a wretch through him has gone to hell.

W. H. DAVIES

The Pond

So innocent, so quiet—yet
   That glitter in the water's eye
Has some strange meaning there, I fear;
   Did waves run wild and butt this bank
With their curled horns, when it happened here?

Beneath these heart-shaped lily-leaves,
   In water, lies a broken heart:
And one white lily in this place—
   In this deep, silent, leaf-bound pond—
Is that dead woman's upturned face.

The Trick

No answer, yet I called her name,
I shook her, but no motion came,
   She showed no signs of having breath;
When, in my fear, the light was sought,
The hussy laughed: "Is this," I thought,—
   "Some strange convulsion after death?"

I could have murdered her that hour,
To think that she had used such power
   In making me betray a love
Secret and vast, and still unknown;
A love half-dreamt, till life is done,
   And only Death himself can prove.

Love's Caution

Tell them, when you are home again,
   How warm the air was now ;

How silent were the birds and leaves,
   And of the moon's full glow;
      And how we saw afar
      A falling star:
It was a tear of pure delight
Ran down the face of Heaven this happy night.

Our kisses are but love in flower,
   Until that greater time
When, gathering strength, those flowers take wing,
   And Love can reach his prime.
      And now, my heart's delight,
      Good night, good night;
Give me the last sweet kiss—
But do not breathe at home one word of this!

WALTER DE LA MARE

In the Dock

Pallid, mis-shapen he stands. The World's grimed thumb,
Now hooked securely in his matted hair,
Has haled him struggling from his poisonous slum
And flung him, mute as fish, close-netted there.
His bloodless hands entalon that iron rail.
He gloats in beastlike trance. His settling eyes
From staring face to face rove on—and quail.
Justice for carrion pants; and these the flies.
Voice after voice in smooth impartial drone
Erects horrific in his darkening brain
A timber framework, where agape, alone
Bright life will kiss good-bye the cheek of Cain.
Sudden like wolf he cries; and sweats to see
When howls man's soul, it howls inaudibly.

WALTER DE LA MARE

To a Candle

Burn stilly, thou; and come with me.
I'll screen thy rays. Now . . . Look, and see,
Where, like a flower furled,
Sealed from this busy world,
Tranquil brow, and lid, and lip,
One I love lies here asleep.

Low upon her pillow is
A head of such strange loveliness—
Gilded-brown, unwoven hair—
That dread springs up to see it there:
Lest so profound a trance should be
Death's momentary alchemy.

Venture closer, then. Thy light
Be little day to this small night!
Fretting through her lids it makes
The lashes stir on those pure cheeks;
The scarcely-parted lips, it seems,
Pine, but in vain, to tell her dreams.

Every curve and hollow shows
In faintest shadow—mouth and nose;
Pulsing beneath the silken skin
The milk-blue blood rills out and in:
A bird's might be that slender bone,
Magic itself to ponder on.

Time hath spread its nets in vain;
The child she was is home again;
Veiled with Sleep's seraphic grace,
How innocent yet how wise a face!
Mutely entreating, it seems to sigh,—
"Love made me. It is only I.

"Love made this house wherein there dwells
A thing divine, and homeless else.
Not mine the need to ponder why
In this sweet prison I exult and sigh.
Not mine to bid you hence. God knows
It was for joy he shaped the rose."

See, she stirs. A hand at rest
Slips from above that gentle breast,
White as winter-mounded snows,
Summer-sweet as that wild rose . . .
Thou lovely thing! Ah, welladay!
Candle, I dream. Come, come away!

At Ease

Most wounds can Time repair;
    But some are mortal—these:
For a broken heart there is no balm,
    No cure for a heart at ease—

At ease, but cold as stone,
    Though the intellect spin on,
And the feat and practised face may show
    Nought of the life that is gone;

But smiles, as by habit taught;
    And sighs, as by custom led;
And the soul within is safe from damnation,
        Since it is dead.

The Ghost

"Who knocks?" "I, who was beautiful,
    Beyond all dreams to restore,
I, from the roots of the dark thorn am hither.
    And knock on the door."

"Who speaks?" "I—once was my speech
   Sweet as the bird's on the air,
When echo lurks by the waters to heed;
   'Tis I speak thee fair."

"Dark is the hour!" "Ay, and cold."
   "Lone is my house." "Ah, but mine?"
"Sight, touch, lips, eyes yearned in vain."
   "Long dead these to thine . . ."

Silence. Still faint on the porch
   Brake the flames of the stars.
In gloom groped a hope-wearied hand
   Over keys, bolts, and bars.

A face peered. All the grey night
   In chaos of vacancy shone;
Nought but vast sorrow was there—
   The sweet cheat gone.

The Railway Junction

From here through tunnelled gloom the track
Forks into two; and one of these
Wheels onward into darkening hills,
And one toward distant seas.

How still it is; the signal light
At set of sun shines palely green;
A thrush sings; other sound there's none,
Nor traveller to be seen—

Where late there was a throng. And now
In peace awhile, I sit alone;
Though soon, at the appointed hour,
I shall myself be gone.

But not their way: the bow-legged groom,
The parson in black, the widow and son,
The sailor with his cage, the gaunt
Gamekeeper with his gun,

That fair one, too, discreetly veiled—
All, who so mutely came, and went,
Will reach those far nocturnal hills,
Or shores, ere night is spent.

I nothing know why thus we met—
Their thoughts, their longings, hopes, their fate:
And what shall I remember, except—
The evening growing late—

That here through tunnelled gloom the track
Forks into two; of these
One into darkening hills leads on,
And one toward distant seas?

JOHN MASEFIELD

from *Lollingdon Downs*

I could not sleep for thinking of the sky,
The unending sky, with all its million suns
Which turn their planets everlastingly
In nothing, where the fire-haired comet runs.
If I could sail that nothing, I should cross
Silence and emptiness with dark stars passing;
Then, in the darkness, see a point of gloss
Burn to a glow, and glare, and keep amassing,
And rage into a sun with wandering planets,
And drop behind; and then, as I proceed,
See his last light upon his last moon's granites
Die to a dark that would be night indeed:
Night where my soul might sail a million years
To nothing, not even Death, not even tears.

46

JOHN MASEFIELD

Wood-Pigeons

Often the woodman scares them as he comes
Swinging his axe to split the fallen birch:
The keeper with his nim-nosed dog at search
Flushes them unaware; then the hive hums.

Then from the sheddings underneath the beech,
Where squirrels rout, the flock of pigeons goes,
Their wings like sticks in battle giving blows,
The hundred hurtling to be out of reach.

Their wings flash white above a darker fan,
In drifts the colour of the smoke they pass,
They disappear above the valley grass,
They re-appear against the woodland tan.

Now that the valley woodlands are all bare,
Their flocks drift daily thus, now up, now down,
Blue-grey against the sodden of the brown,
Grey-blue against the twig-tips, thin in air.

It is a beauty none but Autumn has,
These drifts of blue-grey birds whom Nature binds
Into communities of single minds,
From early leaf-fall until Candlemas.

So in the failing Life when Death and Dread,
With axe and mongrel stalk the withering wood,
The pigeons of the spirit's solitude
Clatter to glory at the stealthy tread,

And each, made deathless by the Spirit's joy,
Launch from the leaves that have forgotten green,
And from the valley seek another scene,
That Dread can darken not, nor Death destroy.

47

EDWARD THOMAS

Old Man

Old Man, or Lad's-Love,—in the name there's nothing
To one that knows not Lad's-Love, or Old Man,
The hoar-green feathery herb, almost a tree,
Growing with rosemary and lavender.
Even to one that knows it well, the names
Half decorate, half perplex, the thing it is:
At least, what that is clings not to the names
In spite of time. And yet I like the names.

The herb itself I like not, but for certain
I love it, as some day the child will love it
Who plucks a feather from the door-side bush
Whenever she goes in or out of the house.
Often she waits there, snipping the tips and shrivelling
The shreds at last on to the path,
Thinking, perhaps of nothing, till she sniffs
Her fingers and runs off. The bush is still
But half as tall as she, though it is as old;
So well she clips it. Not a word she says;
And I can only wonder how much hereafter
She will remember, with that bitter scent,
Of garden rows, and ancient damson trees
Topping a hedge, a bent path to a door,
A low thick bush beside the door, and me
Forbidding her to pick.

                 As for myself,
Where first I met the bitter scent is lost.
I, too, often shrivel the grey shreds,
Sniff them and think and sniff again and try
Once more to think what it is I am remembering,
Always in vain. I cannot like the scent,
Yet I would rather give up others more sweet,
With no meaning, than this bitter one.

I have mislaid the key. I sniff the spray
And think of nothing; I see and I hear nothing;
Yet seem, too, to be listening, lying in wait
For what I should, yet never can, remember:
No garden appears, no path, no hoar-green bush
Of Lad's-Love, or Old Man, no child beside,
Neither father nor mother, nor any playmate;
Only an avenue, dark, nameless, without end.

Aspens

All day and night, save winter, every weather,
Above the inn, the smithy, and the shop,
The aspens at the cross-roads talk together
Of rain, until their last leaves fall from the top.

Out of the blacksmith's cavern comes the ringing
Of hammer, shoe, and anvil; out of the inn
The clink, the hum, the roar, the random singing—
The sounds that for these fifty years have been.

The whisper of the aspens is not drowned,
And over lightless pane and footless road,
Empty as sky, with every other sound
Not ceasing, calls their ghosts from their abode.

A silent smithy, a silent inn, nor fails
In the bare moonlight or the thick-furred gloom,
In tempest or the night of nightingales,
To turn the cross-roads to a ghostly room.

And it would be the same were no house near.
Over all sorts of weather, men, and times,
Aspens must shake their leaves and men may hear
But need not listen, more than to my rhymes.

49

Whatever wind blows, while they and I have leaves
We cannot other than an aspen be
That ceaselessly, unreasonably grieves,
Or so men think who like a different tree.

October

The green elm with the one great bough of gold
Lets leaves into the grass slip, one by one,—
The short hill grass, the mushrooms small, milk-white,
Harebell and scabious and tormentil,
That blackberry and gorse, in dew and sun,
Bow down to; and the wind travels too light
To shake the fallen birch leaves from the fern;
The gossamers wander at their own will.
At heavier steps than birds' the squirrels scold.
The late year has grown fresh again and new
As Spring and to the touch is not more cool
Than it is warm to the gaze; and now I might
As happy be as earth is beautiful,
Were I some other or with earth could turn
In alternation of violet and rose,
Harebell and snowdrop, at their season due,
And gorse that has no time not to be gay.
But if this be not happiness,—who knows?
Some day I shall think this a happy day,
And this mood by the name of melancholy
Shall no more blackened and obscurèd be.

The Gallows

There was a weasel lived in the sun
With all his family,
Till a keeper shot him with his gun
And hung him up on a tree,
Where he swings in the wind and rain,
In the sun and in the snow,
Without pleasure, without pain,
On the dead oak tree bough.

There was a crow who was no sleeper,
But a thief and a murderer
Till a very late hour; and this keeper
Made him one of the things that were,
To hang and flap in rain and wind,
In the sun and in the snow.
There are no more sins to be sinned
On the dead oak tree bough.

There was a magpie, too,
Had a long tongue and a long tail;
He could both talk and do—
But what did that avail?
He, too, flaps in the wind and rain
Alongside weasel and crow,
Without pleasure, without pain,
On the dead oak tree bough.

And many other beasts
And birds, skin, bone and feather,
Have been taken from their feasts
And hung up there together,
To swing and have endless leisure
In the sun and in the snow,
Without pain, without pleasure,
On the dead oak tree bough.

Two Houses

Between a sunny bank and the sun
The farmhouse smiles
On the riverside plat:
No other one
So pleasant to look at
And remember, for many miles,
So velvet hushed and cool under the warm tiles.

Not far from the road it lies, yet caught
Far out of reach
Of the road's dust
And the dusty thought
Of passers-by, though each
Stops, and turns, and must
Look down at it like a wasp at the muslined peach.

But another house stood there long before:
And as if above graves
Still the turf heaves
Above its stones:
Dark hangs the sycamore,
Shadowing kennel and bones
And the black dog that shakes his chain and moans.

And when he barks, over the river
Flashing fast,
Dark echoes reply,
And the hollow past
Half yields the dead that never
More than half hidden lie:
And out they creep and back again for ever.

No One So Much As You

No one so much as you
Loves this my clay,
Or would lament as you
Its dying day.

You know me through and through
Though I have not told,
And though with what you know
You are not bold.

EDWARD THOMAS

None ever was so fair
As I thought you:
Not a word can I bear
Spoken against you.

All that I ever did
For you seemed coarse
Compared with what I hid
Nor put in force.

My eyes scarce dare meet you
Lest they should prove
I but respond to you
And do not love.

We look and understand,
We cannot speak
Except in trifles and
Words the most weak.

For I at most accept
Your love, regretting
That is all: I have kept
Only a fretting

That I could not return
All that you gave
And could not ever burn
With the love you have,

Till sometimes it did seem
Better it were
Never to see you more
Than linger here

With only gratitude
Instead of love—
A pine in solitude
Cradling a dove.

HAROLD MONRO

Midnight Lamentation

When you and I go down
Breathless and cold,
Our faces both worn back
To earthly mould,
How lonely we shall be!
What shall we do,
You without me,
I without you?

I cannot bear the thought
You, first, may die,
Nor of how you will weep,
Should I.
We are too much alone;
What can we do
To make our bodies one:
You, me; I, you?

We are most nearly born
Of one same kind;
We have the same delight,
The same true mind.
Must we then part, we part;
Is there no way
To keep a beating heart,
And light of day?

I could now rise and run
Through street on street
To where you are breathing—you,
That we might meet,
And that your living voice
Might sound above
Fear, and we two rejoice
Within our love.

HAROLD MONRO

How frail the body is,
And we are made
As only in decay
To lean and fade.
I think too much of death;
There is a gloom
When I can't hear your breath
Calm in some room.

O but how suddenly
Either may droop;
Countenance be so white,
Body stoop.
Then there may be a place
Where fading flowers
Drop on a lifeless face
Through weeping hours.

Is then nothing safe?
Can we not find
Some everlasting life
In our one mind?
I feel it like disgrace
Only to understand
Your spirit through your word,
Or by your hand.

I cannot find a way
Through love and through;
I cannot reach beyond
Body, to you.
When you or I must go
Down evermore,
There'll be no more to say
—But a locked door.

JOHN FREEMAN

Caterpillars

Of caterpillars Fabre tells how day after day
Around the rim of a vast earth pot they crawled,
Tricked thither as they filed shuffling out one morn
Head to tail when the common hunger called.

Head to tail in a heaving ring day after day,
Night after slow night, the starving mommets crept,
Each following each, head to tail, day after day,
An unbroken ring of hunger—then it was snapt.

I thought of you, long-heaving, horned green caterpillars,
As I lay awake. My thoughts crawled each after each,
Crawling at night each after each on the same nerve,
An unbroken ring of thoughts too sore for speech.

Over and over and over and over again
The same hungry thoughts and the same hopeless regrets,
Over and over again the same truths, again and again
In a heaving ring returning the same regrets.

D. H. LAWRENCE

A Young Wife

The pain of loving you
Is almost more than I can bear.

I walk in fear of you.
The darkness starts up where
You stand, and the night comes through
Your eyes when you look at me.

Ah never before did I see
The shadows that live in the sun!

Now every tall glad tree
Turns round its back to the sun
And looks down on the ground, to see
The shadow it used to shun.

At the foot of each glowing thing
A night lies looking up.

Oh, and I want to sing
And dance, but I can't lift up
My eyes from the shadows: dark
They lie spilt round the cup.

What is it?—Hark
The faint fine seethe in the air!

Like the seething sound in a shell!
It is death still seething where
The wild-flower shakes its bell
And the skylark twinkles blue—

The pain of loving you
Is almost more than I can bear.

Song of a Man Who Has Come Through

Not I, not I, but the wind that blows through me!
A fine wind is blowing the new direction of Time.
If only I let it bear me, carry me, if only it carry me!
If only I am sensitive, subtle, oh delicate, a winged gift!
If only, most lovely of all, I yield myself and am borrowed
By the fine, fine wind that takes its course through the chaos of
   the world
Like a fine, an exquisite chisel, a wedge-blade inserted;

If only I am keen and hard like the sheer lip of a wedge
Driven by invisible blows,
The rock will split, we shall come at the wonder, we shall find
   the Hesperides.

Oh, for the wonder that bubbles into my soul,
I would be a good fountain, a good well-head,
Would blur no whisper, spoil no expression.

What is the knocking?
What is the knocking at the door in the night?
It is somebody wants to do us harm.

No, no, it is the three strange angels.
Admit them, admit them.

Tortoise Family Connections

On he goes, the little one,
Bud of the universe,
Pediment of life.

Setting off somewhere, apparently.
Whither away, brisk egg?

His mother deposited him on the soil as if he were no more than
   droppings,
And now he scuffles tinily past her as if she were an old rusty tin.

A mere obstacle,
He veers round the slow great mound of her—
Tortoises always foresee obstacles.

It is no use my saying to him in an emotional voice:
"This is your Mother, she laid you when you were an egg."

He does not even trouble to answer: "Woman, what have I to
   do with thee?"
He wearily looks the other way,
And she even more wearily looks another way still,
Each with the utmost apathy,
Incognisant,
Unaware,
Nothing.

As for papa,
He snaps when I offer him his offspring,
Just as he snaps when I poke a bit of stick at him,
Because he is irascible this morning, an irascible tortoise
Being touched with love, and devoid of fatherliness.

Father and mother,
And three little brothers,
And all rambling aimless, like little perambulating pebbles
   scattered in the garden,
Not knowing each other from bits of earth or old tins.

Except that papa and mama are old acquaintances, of course,
Though family feeling there is none, not even the beginnings.

Fatherless, motherless, brotherless, sisterless
Little tortoise.

Row on then, small pebble,
Over the clods of the autumn, wind-chilled sunshine,
Young gaiety.

Does he look for a companion?

No, no, don't think it.
He doesn't know he is alone;
Isolation is his birthright,
This atom.

To row forward, and reach himself tall on spiny toes,
To travel, to burrow into a little loose earth, afraid of the night,
To crop a little substance,
To move, and to be quite sure that he is moving:
Basta!
To be a tortoise!
Think of it, in a garden of inert clods
A brisk, brindled little tortoise, all to himself—
Adam!

In a garden of pebbles and insects
To roam, and feel the slow heart beat
Tortoise-wise, the first bell sounding
From the warm blood, in the dark-creation morning.

Moving, and being himself,
Slow, and unquestioned,
And inordinately there, O stoic!
Wandering in the slow triumph of his own existence,
Ringing the soundless bell of his presence in chaos,
And biting the frail grass arrogantly,
Decidedly arrogantly.

Sicilian Cyclamens

When he pushed his bush of black hair off his brow:
When she lifted her mop from her eyes, and screwed it in a knob
    behind
        —O act of fearful temerity!
When they felt their foreheads bare, naked to heaven, their eyes
    revealed:
When they felt the light of heaven brandished like a knife at
    their defenceless eyes,
And the sea like a blade at their face,
Mediterranean savages:
When they came out, face-revealed, under heaven, from the
    shaggy undergrowth of their own hair

For the first time,
They saw the tiny rose cyclamens between their toes, growing
Where the slow toads sat brooding on the past.

Slow toads, and cyclamen leaves
Stickily glistening with eternal shadow
Keeping to earth.
Cyclamen leaves
Toad-filmy, earth-iridescent
Beautiful
Frost-filigreed
Spumed with mud
Snail-nacreous
Low down.

The shaking aspect of the sea
And man's defenceless bare face
And cyclamens putting their ears back.

Long, pensive, slim-muzzled greyhound buds
Dreamy, not yet present,
Drawn out of earth
At his toes.

Dawn-rose
Sub-delighted, stone-engendered
Cyclamens, young cyclamens
Arching
Waking, pricking their ears
Like delicate very-young greyhound bitches
Half-yawning at the open, inexperienced
Vista of day,
Folding back their soundless petalled ears.

Greyhound bitches
Bending their rosy muzzles pensive down,
And breathing soft, unwilling to wake to the new day
Yet sub-delighted.

D. H. LAWRENCE

Ah Mediterranean morning, when our world began!
Far-off Mediterranean mornings,
Pelasgic faces uncovered,
And unbudding cyclamens.

The hare suddenly goes uphill
Laying back her long ears with unwinking bliss.

And up the pallid, sea-blanched Mediterranean stone-slopes
Rose cyclamen, ecstatic fore-runner!
Cyclamens, ruddy-muzzled cyclamens
In little bunches like bunches of wild hares
Muzzles together, ears-aprick,
Whispering witchcraft
Like women at a well, the dawn-fountain.

Greece, and the world's morning
Where all the Parthenon marbles still fostered the roots of the
    cyclamen.
Violets
Pagan, rosy-muzzled violets
Autumnal
Dawn-pink,
Dawn-pale
Among squat toad-leaves sprinkling the unborn
Erechtheion marbles.

ANDREW YOUNG

Field-Glasses

Though buds still speak in hints
And frozen ground has set the flints
As fast as precious stones
And birds perch on the boughs, silent as cones,

ANDREW YOUNG

Suddenly waked from sloth
Young trees put on a ten years' growth
And stones double their size,
Drawn nearer through field-glasses' greater eyes.

Why I borrow their sight
Is not to give small birds a fright
Creeping up close by inches;
I make the trees come, bringing tits and finches.

I lift a field itself
As lightly as I might a shelf,
And the rooks do not rage
Caught for a moment in my crystal cage.

And while I stand and look,
Their private lives an open book,
I feel so privileged
My shoulders prick, as though they were half-fledged.

Wiltshire Downs

The cuckoo's double note
Loosened like bubbles from a drowning throat
Floats through the air
In mockery of pipit, lark and stare.

The stable-boys thud by
Their horses slinging divots at the sky
And with bright hooves
Printing the sodden turf with lucky grooves.

As still as a windhover
A shepherd in his flapping coat leans over
His tall sheep-crook
And shearlings, tegs and yoes cons like a book.

And one tree-crowned long barrow
Stretched like a sow that has brought forth her farrow
Hides a king's bones
Lying like broken sticks among the stones.

The Flood

The winter flood is out, dully glazing the weald,
The Adur, a drowned river, lies in its bed concealed;
Fishes flowing through fences explore paddock and field.

Bushes, waist-deep in water, stand sprinkled here and there;
A solitary gate, as though hung in mid-air,
Waits idly open, leading from nowhere to nowhere.

These bushes at night-fall will have strange fish for guests,
That wagtail, tit and warbler darkened with their nests;
Where flood strays now, light-headed lapwings lifted crests.

But soon comes spring again; the hazel-boughs will angle
With bait of yellow catkins that in the loose winds dangle
And starry scarlet blossoms their blind buds bespangle;

Dogs'-mercury from the earth unfold seed-clasping fists
And green-leaved honeysuckle roll in tumbling twists
And dreams of spring shake all the seeds that sleep in cists.

O blue-eyed one, too well I know you will not awake,
Who waked or lay awake so often for my sake,
Nor would I ask our last leave-taking to retake.

If lesser love of flower or bird waken my song,
It is that greater love, too full to flow along,
Falls like that Adur back, flood-like, silent and strong.

FRANCES CORNFORD

Summer Beach

For how long known this boundless wash of light;
This smell of purity; this gleaming waste;
This wind? This brown, strewn wrack how old a sight,
These pebbles round to touch and salt to taste?

See, the slow, marbled heave, the liquid arch,
Before the waves' procession to the land
Flowers in foam; the ripples onward march;
Their last caresses on the pure hard sand.

For how long known these bleaching corks, new-made,
Smooth and enchanted from the lapping sea?
Since first I laboured with a wooden spade
Against the background of Eternity.

SIEGFRIED SASSOON

Prelude: The Troops

Dim, gradual thinning of the shapeless gloom
Shudders to drizzling daybreak that reveals
Disconsolate men who stamp their sodden boots
And turn dulled, sunken faces to the sky
Haggard and hopeless. They, who have beaten down
The stale despair of night, must now renew
Their desolation in the truce of dawn,
Murdering the livid hours that grope for peace.

Yet these, who cling to life with stubborn hands,
Can grin through storms of death and find a gap
In the clawed, cruel tangles of his defence.

They march from safety, and the bird-sung joy
Of grass-green thickets, to the land where all
Is ruin, and nothing blossoms but the sky
That hastens over them where they endure
Sad, smoking, flat horizons, reeking woods,
And foundered trench-lines volleying doom for doom.

O my brave brown companions, when your souls
Flock silently away, and the eyeless dead
Shame the wild beast of battle on the ridge,
Death will stand grieving in that field of war
Since your unvanquished hardihood is spent.
And through some mooned Valhalla there will pass
Battalions and battalions, scarred from hell;
The unreturning army that was youth;
The legions who have suffered and are dust.

At the Grave of Henry Vaughan

Above the voiceful windings of a river
An old green slab of simply graven stone
Shuns notice, overshadowed by a yew.
Here Vaughan lies dead, whose name flows on for ever
Through pastures of the spirit washed with dew
And starlit with eternities unknown.

Here sleeps the Silurist; the loved physician;
The face that left no portraiture behind;
The skull that housed white angels and had vision
Of daybreak through the gateways of the mind.
   Here faith and mercy, wisdom and humility
   (Whose influence shall prevail for evermore)
   Shine. And this lowly grave tells Heaven's tranquillity.
   And here stand I, a suppliant at the door.

SIEGFRIED SASSOON

I Stood with the Dead

I stood with the Dead, so forsaken and still:
When dawn was grey I stood with the Dead.
And my slow heart said, "You must kill, you must kill:
Soldier, soldier, morning is red."

On the shapes of the slain in their crumpled disgrace
I stared for a while through the thin cold rain . . .
"O lad that I loved, there is rain on your face,
And your eyes are blurred and sick like the plain."

I stood with the Dead . . . They were dead; they were dead;
My heart and my head beat a march of dismay:
And gusts of the wind came dulled by the guns.
"Fall in!" I shouted; "Fall in for your pay!"

EDWIN MUIR

The Combat

It was not meant for human eyes,
That combat on the shabby patch
Of clods and trampled turf that lies
Somewhere beneath the sodden skies
For eye of toad or adder to catch.

And having seen it I accuse
The crested animal in his pride,
Arrayed in all the royal hues
Which hide the claws he well can use
To tear the heart out of the side.

Body of leopard, eagle's head
And whetted beak, and lion's mane,
And frost-grey hedge of feathers spread
Behind—he seemed of all things bred.
I shall not see his like again.

67

As for his enemy, there came in
A soft round beast as brown as clay;
All rent and patched his wretched skin;
A battered bag he might have been,
Some old used thing to throw away.

Yet he awaited face to face
The furious beast and the swift attack.
Soon over and done. That was no place
Or time for chivalry or for grace.
The fury had him on his back.

And two small paws like hands flew out
To right and left as the trees stood by.
One would have said beyond a doubt
This was the very end of the bout,
But that the creature would not die.

For ere the death-stroke he was gone,
Writhed, whirled, huddled into his den,
Safe somehow there. The fight was done,
And he had lost who had all but won.
But oh his deadly fury then.

A while the place lay blank, forlorn,
Drowsing as in relief from pain.
The cricket chirped, the grating thorn
Stirred, and a little sound was born.
The champions took their posts again.

And all began. The stealthy paw
Slashed out and in. Could nothing save
Those rags and tatters from the claw?
Nothing. And yet I never saw
A beast so helpless and so brave.

And now, while the trees stand watching, still
The unequal battle rages there.
The killing beast that cannot kill
Swells and swells in his fury till
You'd almost think it was despair.

EDWIN MUIR

The Child Dying

Unfriendly, friendly universe,
I pack your stars into my purse,
And bid you, bid you so farewell.
That I can leave you, quite go out,
Go out, go out beyond all doubt,
My father says, is the miracle.

You are so great, and I so small:
I am nothing, you are all:
Being nothing, I can take this way.
Oh I need neither rise nor fall,
For when I do not move at all
I shall be out of all your day.

It's said some memory will remain
In the other place, grass in the rain,
Light on the land, sun on the sea,
A flitting grace, a phantom face,
But the world is out. There is no place
Where it and its ghost can ever be.

Father, father, I dread this air
Blown from the far side of despair,
The cold cold corner. What house, what hold,
What hand is there? I look and see
Nothing-filled eternity,
And the great round world grows weak and old.

Hold my hand, oh hold it fast—
I am changing!—until at last
My hand in yours no more will change,
Though yours change on. You here, I there,
So hand in hand, twin-leafed despair—
I did not know death was so strange.

EDWIN MUIR

The Face

See me with all the terrors on my roads,
The crusted shipwrecks rotting in my seas,
And the untroubled oval of my face
That alters idly with the moonlike modes
And is unfathomably framed to please
And deck the angular bone with passing grace.

I should have worn a terror-mask, should be
A sight to frighten hope and faith away,
Half charnel field, half battle and rutting ground.
Instead I am a smiling summer sea
That sleeps while underneath from bound to bound
The sun- and star-shaped killers gorge and play.

The Killing

That was the day they killed the Son of God
On a squat hill-top by Jerusalem.
Zion was bare, her children from their maze
Sucked by the demon curiosity
Clean through the gates. The very halt and blind
Had somehow got themselves up to the hill.

After the ceremonial preparation,
The scourging, nailing, nailing against the wood,
Erection of the main-trees with their burden,
While from the hill rose an orchestral wailing,
They were there at last, high up in the soft spring day.
We watched the writhings, heard the moanings, saw
The three heads turning on their separate axles
Like broken wheels left spinning. Round *his* head
Was loosely bound a crown of plaited thorn
That hurt at random, stinging temple and brow
As the pain swung into its envious circle.

EDWIN MUIR

In front the wreath was gathered in a knot
That as he gazed looked like the last stump left
Of a death-wounded deer's great antlers. Some
Who came to stare grew silent as they looked,
Indignant or sorry. But the hardened old
And the hard-hearted young, although at odds
From the first morning, cursed him with one curse,
Having prayed for a Rabbi or an armed Messiah
And found the Son of God. What use to them
Was a God or a Son of God? Of what avail
For purposes such as theirs? Beside the cross-foot,
Alone, four women stood and did not move
All day. The sun revolved, the shadow wheeled,
The evening fell. His head lay on his breast,
But in his breast they watched his heart move on
By itself alone, accomplishing its journey.
Their taunts grew louder, sharpened by the knowledge
That he was walking in the park of death,
Far from their rage. Yet all grew stale at last,
Spite, curiosity, envy, hate itself.
They waited only for death and death was slow
And came so quietly they scarce could mark it.
They were angry then with death and death's deceit.

I was a stranger, could not read these people
Or this outlandish deity. Did a God
Indeed in dying cross my life that day
By chance, he on his road and I on mine?

EDITH SITWELL

Still Falls the Rain

(The Raids 1940. Night and Dawn)

Still falls the Rain—
Dark as the world of man, black as our loss—
Blind as the nineteen hundred and forty nails
Upon the Cross.

Still falls the Rain
With a sound like the pulse of the heart that is changed to the
    hammer-beat
In the Potter's Field, and the sound of the impious feet

On the Tomb:
               Still falls the Rain
In the Field of Blood where the small hopes breed and the human
    brain
Nurtures its greed, that worm with the brow of Cain.

Still falls the Rain
At the feet of the Starved Man hung upon the Cross.
Christ that each day, each night, nails there, have mercy on us—

On Dives and on Lazarus:
Under the Rain the sore and the gold are as one.

Still falls the Rain—
Still falls the Blood from the Starved Man's wounded Side:
He bears in His Heart all wounds,—those of the light that died,
The last faint spark
In the self-murdered heart, the wounds of the sad uncompre-
    hending dark,
The wounds of the baited bear,—
The blind and weeping bear whom the keepers beat
On his helpless flesh . . . the tears of the hunted hare.

Still falls the Rain—
Then—O Ile leape up to my God: who pulles me doune—
See, see where Christ's blood streames in the firmament:
It flows from the Brow we nailed upon the tree
Deep to the dying, to the thirsting heart
That holds the fires of the world—dark-smirched with pain
As Caesar's laurel crown.

Then sounds the voice of One who like the heart of man
Was once a child who among beasts has lain—
"Still do I love, still shed my innocent light, my Blood, for thee."

Lullaby

Though the world has slipped and gone,
Sounds my loud discordant cry
Like the steel birds' song on high:
"Still one thing is left—the Bone!"
Then out danced the Babioun.

She sat in the hollow of the sea—
A socket whence the eye's put out—
She sang to the child a lullaby
(The steel birds' nest was thereabout).

"Do, do, do, do—
Thy mother's hied to the vaster race:
The Pterodactyl made its nest
And laid a steel egg in her breast—
Under the Judas-coloured sun.
She'll work no more, nor dance, nor moan,
And I am come to take her place
Do, do.

There's nothing left but earth's low bed—
(The Pterodactyl fouls its nest):
But steel wings fan thee to thy rest,
And wingless truth and larvae lie
And eyeless hope and handless fear—
All these for thee as toys are spread,
Do—do—

Red is the bed of Poland, Spain,
And thy mother's breast, who has grown wise
In that fouled nest. If she could rise,
Give birth again,

In wolfish pelt she'd hide thy bones
To shield thee from the world's long cold,
And down on all fours shouldst thou crawl
For thus from no height canst thou fall—
Do, do.

She'd give no hands: there's nought to hold
And nought to make: there's dust to sift,
But no food for the hands to lift.
Do, do.

Heed my ragged lullaby,
Fear not living, fear not chance;
All is equal—blindness, sight,
There is no depth, there is no height:
Do, do.

The Judas-coloured sun is gone,
And with the Ape thou art alone—
Do,
     Do."

NOTE.—The phrase "out-dance the Babioun" occurs in an epigram
by Ben Johnson.

Heart and Mind

Said the Lion to the Lioness—"When you are amber dust—
No more a raging fire like the heat of the Sun
(No liking but all lust)—
Remember still the flowering of the amber blood and bone,
The rippling of bright muscles like a sea,
Remember the rose-prickles of bright paws,
Though we shall mate no more
Till the fire of that sun the heart and the moon-cold bone are
    one."

Said the Skeleton lying upon the sands of Time—
"The great gold planet that is the mourning heat of the Sun
Is greater than all gold, more powerful
Than the tawny body of a Lion that fire consumes
Like all that grows or leaps . . . so is the heart
More powerful than all dust. Once I was Hercules
Or Samson, strong as the pillars of the seas:
But the flames of the heart consumed me, and the mind
Is but a foolish wind."

Said the Sun to the Moon—"When you are but a lonely white
   crone,
And I, a dead King in my golden armour somewhere in a dark
   wood,
Remember only this of our hopeless love
That never till Time is done
Will the fire of the heart and the fire of the mind be one."

Song

Once my heart was a summer rose
That cares not for right or wrong,
And the sun was another rose, that year,
They shone, the sun and the rose, my dear—
Over the long and the light summer land
All the bright summer long.

As I walked in the long and the light summer land
All that I knew of shade
Was the cloud, my ombrelle of rustling grey
Sharp silk, it had spokes of grey steel rain—
Hiding my rose away, my dear,
Hiding my rose away.

And my laughter shone like a flight of birds
All in the summer gay,—
Tumbling pigeons and chattering starlings
And other pretty darlings, my dear,
And other pretty darlings.

To my heart like a rose, a rain of tears
(All the bright summer long)
Was only the sheen on a wood-dove's breast,
And sorrow only her song, my love—
And sorrow only my rest.

I passed a while in Feather Town—
(All the bright summer long)—
The idle wind puffed that town up
In air, then blew it down.

I walk alone now in Lead Town
(All in the summer gay . . .)
Where the steady people walk like the Dead—
And will not look my way.

For, withering my heart, that summer rose,
Came another heart like a sun—
And it drank all the dew from the rose, my love,
And the birds have forgotten their song
That sounded all summer long, my dear—
All the bright summer long.

Sailor, What of the Isles?

To Millicent Huddleston Rogers

"Sailor, what of the isles—
The green worlds grown
From a little seed? What of the islands known and those
  unknown?"

"I have returned over the long and lonely sea;
And only human need
For the world of men is mine; I have forgot Immensity.

The rustling sea was a green world of leaves;
The isle of Hispaniola in its form
Was like the leaf of a chestnut tree in June.
And there is the gold region—the gold falls like rain with a long
  and leafy tune.

An old man bore us lumps of gold . . . the small,
Like walnuts husked with earth; the great,
As large as oranges, and leafy earth
Still clung to them. And when you thought that fireflies lit the
  night,
These were but nuggets, lying on the dark earth, burning
  bright."

"Sailor, what of the maps of the known world?" "The old
    Chinese,
Whose talk was like the sound of June leaves drinking rain,
Constructed maps of the known world—the few
Islands and two countries that they knew.

They thought the heavens were round,
The earth square, and their empire at the earth's centre . . .
    just as you
And I believe we are the world's centre and the stars
Are grown from us as the bright seas in a rind of gold
Are grown from the smooth stem of the orange-tree.

Those maps of the Yellow Empire then were drawn,
As we think, upside down:
Tongking was placed
Where usually the North stands, and Mongolia graced
The South. The names, too, were writ upside down.
For how is it possible, in this flat world, to know
Why South should be below, the North above—
Why man should hold creeds high one moment, the next moment
    low?"

"Sailor, what of the maps of skies? Is that Orion?" "No, the
    sight
Is of a far island. What you see
Is where they are gathering carbuncles, garnets, diamonds
    bright
As fireflies with a gardener's rake under the spice trees and the
    orange trees."

"Sailor, what do you know of this world, my Self . . . a child
Standing before you—or an isle
To which no sail has crossed over the long and lonely sea?
What do you know of this island, of the soil
In which all sainthood or insanity, murder or mockery grows—
    a leafy tree?"

"No more than the gardeners and astronomers who make
Their catalogues of stars for heavens and seeds for garden beds
Know of their green worlds; or the soil, of the great beasts
Whose skin shines like gold fire or fireflies, and whose nostrils
    snort great stars—

The beasts—huge flowers grown from the stem of the green
    darkness; each beast holds
The entire world of plants,
All elements and all the planetary system in
Itself (while the flower holds only the plant-world)
And freed from its stem by light, like the flowers in air—

No more than the father knows of the child, or the sailor of
    chartless isles."

T. S. ELIOT

Sweeney Among the Nightingales

Apeneck Sweeney spreads his knees
Letting his arms hang down to laugh,
The zebra stripes along his jaw
Swelling to maculate giraffe.

The circles of the stormy moon
Slide westward toward the River Plate,
Death and the Raven drift above
And Sweeney guards the horned gate.

Gloomy Orion and the Dog
Are veiled; and hushed the shrunken seas;
The person in the Spanish cape
Tries to sit on Sweeney's knees

Slips and pulls the table cloth
Overturns a coffee-cup,
Reorganised upon the floor
She yawns and draws a stocking up;

The silent man in mocha brown
Sprawls at the window-sill and gapes;
The waiter brings in oranges
Bananas figs and hothouse grapes;

The silent vertebrate in brown
Contracts and concentrates, withdraws;
Rachel *née* Rabinovitch
Tears at the grapes with murderous paws

She and the lady in the cape
Are suspect, thought to be in league;
Therefore the man with heavy eyes
Declines the gambit, shows fatigue,

Leaves the room and reappears
Outside the window, leaning in,
Branches of wistaria
Circumscribe a golden grin;

The host with someone indistinct
Converses at the door apart,
The nightingales are singing near
The Convent of the Sacred Heart,

And sang within the bloody wood
When Agamemnon cried aloud,
And let their liquid siftings fall
To stain the stiff dishonoured shroud.

T. S. ELIOT

Gerontion

Thou hast nor youth nor age
But as it were an after dinner sleep
Dreaming of both.

Here I am, an old man in a dry month,
Being read to by a boy, waiting for rain.
I was neither at the hot gates
Nor fought in the warm rain
Nor knee deep in the salt marsh, heaving a cutlass,
Bitten by flies, fought.
My house is a decayed house,
And the jew squats on the window sill, the owner,
Spawned in some estaminet of Antwerp,
Blistered in Brussels, patched and peeled in London.
The goat coughs at night in the field overhead;
Rocks, moss, stonecrop, iron, merds.
The woman keeps the kitchen, makes tea,
Sneezes at evening, poking the peevish gutter.

                      I an old man,
A dull head among windy spaces.

   Signs are taken for wonders, "We would see a sign"!
The word within a word, unable to speak a word,
Swaddled with darkness. In the juvescence of the year
Came Christ the tiger

   In depraved May, dogwood and chestnut, flowering judas,
To be eaten, to be divided, to be drunk
Among whispers; by Mr Silvero
With caressing hands, at Limoges
Who walked all night in the next room;

By Hakagawa, bowing among the Titians;
By Madame de Tornquist, in the dark room
Shifting the candles; Fraülein von Kulp
Who turned in the hall, one hand on the door. Vacant shuttles
Weave the wind. I have no ghosts,
An old man in a draughty house
Under a windy knob.

After such knowledge, what forgiveness? Think now
History has many cunning passages, contrived corridors
And issues, deceives with whispering ambitions,
Guides us by vanities. Think now
She gives when our attention is distracted
And what she gives, gives with such supple confusions
That the giving famishes the craving. Gives too late
What's not believed in, or if still believed,
In memory only, reconsidered passion. Gives too soon
Into weak hands, what's thought can be dispensed with
Till the refusal propagates a fear. Think
Neither fear nor courage saves us. Unnatural vices
Are fathered by our heroism. Virtues
Are forced upon us by our impudent crimes.
These tears are shaken from the wrath-bearing tree.

    The tiger springs in the new year. Us he devours. Think at last
We have not reached conclusion, when I
Stiffen in a rented house. Think at last
I have not made this show purposelessly
And it is not by any concitation
Of the backward devils.
    I would meet you upon this honestly.
I that was near your heart was removed therefrom
To lose beauty in terror, terror in inquisition.
I have lost my passion: why would I need to keep it
Since what is kept must be adulterated?
I have lost my sight, smell, hearing, taste and touch:
How should I use them for your closer contact?

    These with a thousand small deliberations
Protract the profit of their chilled delirium,
Excite the membrane, when the sense has cooled,
With pungent sauces, multiply variety
In a wilderness of mirrors. What will the spider do,
Suspend its operations, will the weevil
Delay? De Bailhache, Fresca, Mrs Cammel, whirled

Beyond the circuit of the shuddering Bear
In fractured atoms. Gull against the wind, in the windy straits
Of Belle Isle, or running on the Horn,
White feathers in the snow, the Gulf claims,
And an old man driven by the Trades
To a sleepy corner.

                    Tenants of the house,
Thoughts of a dry brain in a dry season.

Marina

Quis hic locus, quae regio, quae mundi plaga?

What seas what shores what grey rocks and what islands
What water lapping the bow
And scent of pine and the woodthrush singing through the fog
What images return
O my daughter.

   Those who sharpen the tooth of the dog, meaning
Death
Those who glitter with the glory of the hummingbird, meaning
Death
Those who sit in the sty of contentment, meaning
Death
Those who suffer the ecstasy of the animals, meaning
Death

Are become unsubstantial, reduced by a wind,
A breath of pine, and the woodsong fog
By this grace dissolved in place

What is this face, less clear and clearer
The pulse in the arm, less strong and stronger—
Given or lent? more distant than stars and nearer than the eye

Whispers and small laughter between leaves and hurrying feet
Under sleep, where all the waters meet.
Bowsprit cracked with ice and paint cracked with heat.
I made this, I have forgotten
And remember.
The rigging weak and the canvas rotten
Between one June and another September.
Made this unknowing, half conscious, unknown, my own.
The garboard strake leaks, the seams need caulking.
This form, this face, this life
Living to live in a world of time beyond me; let me
Resign my life for this life, my speech for that unspoken,
The awakened, lips parted, the hope, the new ships.

What seas what shores what granite islands towards my
      timbers
And woodthrush calling through the fog
My daughter.

East Coker

I

In my beginning is my end. In succession
Houses rise and fall, crumble, are extended,
Are removed, destroyed, restored, or in their place
Is an open field, or a factory, or a by-pass.
Old stone to new building, old timber to new fires,
Old fires to ashes, and ashes to the earth
Which is already flesh, fur and faeces,
Bone of man and beast, cornstalk and leaf.
Houses live and die: there is a time for building
And a time for living and for generation
And a time for the wind to break the loosened pane
And to shake the wainscot where the field-mouse trots
And to shake the tattered arras woven with a silent motto.

In my beginning is my end. Now the light falls
Across the open field, leaving the deep lane

Shuttered with branches, dark in the afternoon,
Where you lean against a bank while a van passes,
And the deep lane insists on the direction
Into the village, in the electric heat
Hypnotised. In a warm haze the sultry light
Is absorbed, not refracted, by grey stone.
The dahlias sleep in the empty silence.
Wait for the early owl.

                    In that open field
If you do not come too close, if you do not come too close,
On a summer midnight, you can hear the music
Of the weak pipe and the little drum
And see them dancing around the bonfire
The association of man and woman
In daunsinge, signifying matrimonie—
A dignified and commodious sacrament.
Two and two, necessarye coniunction,
Holding eche other by the hand or the arm
Whiche betokeneth concorde. Round and round the fire
Leaping through the flames, or joined in circles,
Rustically solemn or in rustic laughter
Lifting heavy feet in clumsy shoes,
Earth feet, loam feet, lifted in country mirth
Mirth of those long since under earth
Nourishing the corn. Keeping time,
Keeping the rhythm in their dancing
As in their living in the living seasons
The time of the seasons and the constellations
The time of milking and the time of harvest
The time of the coupling of man and woman
And that of beasts. Feet rising and falling.
Eating and drinking. Dung and death.

Dawn points, and another day
Prepares for heat and silence. Out at sea the dawn wind
Wrinkles and slides. I am here
Or there, or elsewhere. In my beginning.

II

What is the late November doing
With the disturbance of the spring
And creatures of the summer heat,
And snowdrops writhing under feet
And hollyhocks that aim too high
Red into grey and tumble down
Late roses filled with early snow?
Thunder rolled by the rolling stars
Simulates triumphal cars
Deployed in constellated wars
Scorpion fights against the Sun
Until the Sun and Moon go down
Comets weep and Leonids fly
Hunt the heavens and the plains
Whirled in a vortex that shall bring
The world to that destructive fire
Which burns before the ice-cap reigns.

That was a way of putting it—not very satisfactory:
A periphrastic study in a worn-out poetical fashion,
Leaving one still with the intolerable wrestle
With words and meanings. The poetry does not matter.
It was not (to start again) what one had expected.
What was to be the value of the long looked forward to,
Long hoped for calm, the autumnal serenity
And the wisdom of age? Had they deceived us
Or deceived themselves, the quiet-voiced elders,
Bequeathing us merely a receipt for deceit?
The serenity only a deliberate hebetude,
The wisdom only the knowledge of dead secrets ·
Useless in the darkness into which they peered
Or from which they turned their eyes. There is, it seems to us,
At best, only a limited value
In the knowledge derived from experience.
The knowledge imposes a pattern, and falsifies,
For the pattern is new in every moment

And every moment is a new and shocking
Valuation of all we have been. We are only undeceived
Of that which, deceiving, could no longer harm.
In the middle, not only in the middle of the way
But all the way, in a dark wood, in a bramble,
On the edge of a grimpen, where is no secure foothold,
And menaced by monsters, fancy lights,
Risking enchantment. Do not let me hear
Of the wisdom of old men, but rather of their folly,
Their fear of fear and frenzy, their fear of possession,
Of belonging to another, or to others, or to God.
The only wisdom we can hope to acquire
Is the wisdom of humility: humility is endless.

The houses are all gone under the sea.

The dancers are all gone under the hill.

III

O dark dark dark. They all go into the dark,
The vacant interstellar spaces, the vacant into the vacant:
The captains, merchant bankers, eminent men of letters,
The generous patrons of art, the statesmen and the rulers,
Distinguished civil servants, chairmen of many committees,
Industrial lords and petty contractors, all go into the dark,
And dark the Sun and Moon, and the Almanach de Gotha
And the Stock Exchange Gazette, the Directory of Directors,
And cold the sense and lost the motive of action.
And we all go with them, into the silent funeral,
Nobody's funeral, for there is no one to bury.
I said to my soul, be still, and let the dark come upon you
Which shall be the darkness of God. As, in a theatre,
The lights are extinguished, for the scene to be changed
With a hollow rumble of wings, with a movement of darkness on
    darkness,
And we know that the hills and the trees, the distant panorama
And the bold imposing facade are all being rolled away—
Or as, when an underground train, in the tube, stops too long
    between stations

And the conversation rises and slowly fades into silence
And you see behind every face the mental emptiness deepen
Leaving only the growing terror of nothing to think about;
Or when, under ether, the mind is conscious but conscious of
    nothing—
I said to my soul, be still, and wait without hope
For hope would be hope for the wrong thing; wait without love
For love would be love of the wrong thing; there is yet faith
But the faith and the love and the hope are all in the waiting.
Wait without thought, for you are not ready for thought:
So the darkness shall be the light, and the stillness the dancing
Whisper of running streams, and winter lightning,
The wild thyme unseen and the wild strawberry,
The laughter in the garden, echoed ecstasy
Not lost, but requiring, pointing to the agony
Of death and birth.

            You say I am repeating
Something I have said before. I shall say it again.
Shall I say it again? In order to arrive there,
To arrive where you are, to get from where you are not,
    You must go by a way wherein there is no ecstasy.
In order to arrive at what you do not know
    You must go by a way which is the way of ignorance.
In order to possess what you do not possess
    You must go by the way of dispossession.
In order to arrive at what you are not
    You must go through the way in which you are not.
And what you do not know is the only thing you know
And what you own is what you do not own
And where you are is where you are not.

IV

The wounded surgeon plies the steel
That questions the distempered part;
Beneath the bleeding hands we feel
The sharp compassion of the healer's art
Resolving the enigma of the fever chart.

Our only health is the disease
If we obey the dying nurse
Whose constant care is not to please
But to remind of our, and Adam's curse,
And that, to be restored, our sickness must grow worse.

The whole earth is our hospital
Endowed by the ruined millionaire,
Wherein, if we do well, we shall
Die of the absolute paternal care
That will not leave us, but prevents us everywhere.

The chill ascends from feet to knees,
The fever sings in mental wires.
If to be warmed, then I must freeze
And quake in frigid purgatorial fires
Of which the flame is roses, and the smoke is briars.

The dripping blood our only drink,
The bloody flesh our only food:
In spite of which we like to think
That we are sound, substantial flesh and blood—
Again, in spite of that, we call this Friday good.

V

So here I am, in the middle way, having had twenty years—
Twenty years largely wasted, the years of *l'entre deux guerres*—
Trying to learn to use words, and every attempt
Is a wholly new start, and a different kind of failure
Because one has only learnt to get the better of words
For the thing one no longer has to say, or the way in which
One is no longer disposed to say it. And so each venture
Is a new beginning, a raid on the inarticulate
With shabby equipment always deteriorating
In the general mess of imprecision of feeling,
Undisciplined squads of emotion. And what there is to conquer
By strength and submission, has already been discovered
Once or twice, or several times, by men whom one cannot hope

To emulate—but there is no competition—
There is only the fight to recover what has been lost
And found and lost again and again: and now, under conditions
That seem unpropitious. But perhaps neither gain nor loss.
For us, there is only the trying. The rest is not our business.

Home is where one starts from. As we grow older
The world becomes stranger, the pattern more complicated
Of dead and living. Not the intense moment
Isolated, with no before and after,
But a lifetime burning in every moment
And not the lifetime of one man only
But of old stones that cannot be deciphered.
There is a time for the evening under starlight,
A time for the evening under lamplight
(The evening with the photograph album).
Love is most nearly itself
When here and now cease to matter.
Old men ought to be explorers
Here and there does not matter
We must be still and still moving
Into another intensity
For a further union, a deeper communion
Through the dark cold and the empty desolation,
The wave cry, the wind cry, the vast waters
Of the petrel and the porpoise. In my end is my beginning.

FREDEGOND SHOVE

Sops of Light

Stop still on the stair,
    (Draw in your breath):
Love is the whole air,
    There is no death:

Set the jug aside
  For beams to fill:
Peace is the housetide;
  Then be still.

Let the window stand
  Open to tree;
Light is the whole land
  And the whole sea:
The clocks in the house chime:
  O the day's steep,
But the soul knows no time
  Nor any sleep.

The New Ghost

"And he, casting away his garment, rose and came to Jesus"

And he cast it down, down, on the green grass,
Over the young crocuses, where the dew was—
He cast the garment of his flesh that was full of death,
And like a sword his spirit showed out of the cold sheath.

He went a pace or two, he went to meet his Lord,
And, as I said, his spirit looked like a clean sword,
And seeing him the naked trees began shivering,
And all the birds cried out aloud as it were late spring.

And the Lord came on, He came down and saw
That a soul was waiting there for Him, one without flaw,
And they embraced in the churchyard where the robins play,
And the daffodils hang down their heads, as they burn away.

The Lord held his head fast, and you could see
That he kissed the unsheathed ghost that was gone free—
As a hot sun, on a March day, kisses the cold ground;
And the spirit answered, for he knew well that his peace was
  found.

The spirit trembled, and sprang up at the Lord's word—
As on a wild, April day, springs a small bird—
So the ghost's feet lifting him up, he kissed the Lord's cheek,
And for the greatness of their love neither of them could speak.

But the Lord went then, to show him the way,
Over the young crocuses, under the green may
That was not quite in flower yet—to a far-distant land;
And the ghost followed, like a naked cloud holding the sun's
    hand.

W. J. TURNER

Talking with Soldiers

The mind of the people is like mud,
From which arise strange and beautiful things,
But mud is none the less mud,
Though it bear orchids and prophesying Kings.
Dreams, trees, and water's bright babblings.

It has found form and colour and light,
The cold glimmer of the ice-wrapped Poles;
It has called a far-off glow Arcturus,
And some pale weeds, lilies of the valley.

It has imagined Virgil, Helen and Cassandra;
The sack of Troy, and the weeping for Hector—
Rearing stark up 'mid all this beauty
In the thick, dull neck of Ajax.

There is a dark Pine in Lapland,
And the great, figured Horn of the Reindeer
Moving soundlessly across the snow,
Is its twin brother, double-dreamed,
In the mind of a far-off people.

W. J. TURNER

It is strange that a little mud
Should echo with sounds, syllables and letters,
Should rise up and call a mountain Popocatapetl,
And a green-leafed wood Oleander.

These are the ghosts of invisible things;
There is no Lapland, no Helen and no Hector,
And the Reindeer is a darkening of the brain,
And Oleander is but Oleander.

Mary Magdalena and the vine Lachryma Christi,
Were like ghosts up the ghost of Vesuvius,
As I sat and drank wine with the soldiers,
As I sat in the Inn on the mountain,
Watching the shadows in my mind.

The mind of the people is like mud:
Where are the imperishable things,
The ghosts that flicker in the brain—
Silent women, orchids, and prophesying Kings,
Dreams, trees, and water's bright babblings.

DOROTHY WELLESLEY

Horses

Who, in the garden-pony carrying skeps
Of grass or fallen leaves, his knees gone slack,
Round belly, hollow back,
Sees the Mongolian Tarpan of the Steppes?
Or, in the Shire with plaits and feathered feet,
The war-horse like the wind the Tartar knew?
Or, in the Suffolk Punch, spells out anew
The wild grey asses fleet
With stripe from head to tail, and moderate ears?
In cross sea-donkeys, sheltering as storm gathers,
The mountain zebras maned upon the withers,
With round enormous ears?

DOROTHY WELLESLEY

And who in thoroughbreds in stable garb
Of blazoned rug, ranged orderly, will mark
The wistful eyelashes so long and dark,
And call to mind the old blood of the Barb?
And that slim island on whose bare campaigns
Galloped with flying manes
For a King's pleasure, churning surf and scud,
A white Arabian stud?

That stallion, teazer to Hobgoblin, free
And foaled upon a plain of Barbary:
Godolphin Barb, who dragged a cart for hire
In Paris, but became a famous sire,
Covering all lovely mares, and she who threw
Rataplan to the Baron, loveliest shrew;
King Charles's royal mares; the Dodsworth Dam;
And the descendants: Yellow Turk, King Tom;
And Lath out of Roxana, famous foal;
Careless; Eclipse, unbeaten in the race,
With white blaze on his face;
Prunella who was dam to Parasol.

Blood Arab, pony, pedigree, no name,
All horses are the same:
The Shetland stallion stunted by the damp,
Yet filled with self-importance, stout and small;
The Cleveland slow and tall;
New Forests that may ramp
Their lives out, being branded, breeding free
When bluebells turn the forest to a sea,
When mares with foal at foot flee down the glades,
Sheltering in bramble coverts
From mobs of corn-fed lovers;
Or, at the acorn harvest, in stockades
A round-up being afoot, will stand at bay,
Or, making for the heather clearings, splay
Wide-spread towards the bogs by gorse and whin,
Roped as they flounder in
By foresters.

93

DOROTHY WELLESLEY

But hunters as day fails
Will take the short cut home across the fields;
With slackening rein will stoop through darkening
    wealds;
With creaking leathers skirt the swedes and kales;
Patient, adventurous still,
A horse's ears bob on the distant hill;
He starts to hear
A pheasant chuck or whirr, having the fear
In him of ages filled with war or raid,
Night gallop, ambuscade;
Remembering adventures of his kin
With giant winged worms that coiled round mountain
    bases,
And Nordic tales of young gods riding races
Up courses of the rainbow; here, within
The depth of Hampshire hedges, does he dream
How Athens woke, to hear above her roofs
The welkin flash and thunder to the hoofs
Of Dawn's tremendous team?

ISAAC ROSENBERG

If You Are Fire

If you are fire and I am fire,
Who blows the flame apart
So that desire eludes desire
Around one central heart?

A single root and separate bough,
And what blind hands between
That make our longing's mutual glow
As if it had not been?

94

ISAAC ROSENBERG

Love and Lust

No dream of mortal joy;
Yet all the dreamers die.
We wither with our world
To make room for her sky.

O lust! when you lie ravished,
Broken in the dust,
We will call for love in vain,
Finding love was lust.

Soldier: Twentieth Century

I love you, great new Titan!
Am I not you?
Napoleon and Caesar
Out of you grew.

Out of unthinkable torture,
Eyes kissed by death,
Won back to the world again,
Lost and won in a breath,

Cruel men are made immortal,
Out of your pain born.
They have stolen the sun's power
With their feet on your shoulders worn.

Let them shrink from your girth,
That has outgrown the pallid days,
When you slept like Circe's swine,
Or a word in the brain's ways.

ISAAC ROSENBERG

Chagrin

Caught still as Absalom,
Surely the air hangs
From the swayless cloud-boughs,
Like hair of Absalom
Caught and hanging still.

From the imagined weight
Of spaces in a sky
Of mute chagrin, my thoughts
Hang like branch-clung hair
To trunks of silence swung,
With the choked soul weighing down
Into thick emptiness.
Christ! end this hanging death,
For endlessness hangs therefrom.

Invisibly—branches break
From invisible trees—
The cloud-woods where we rush,
Our eyes holding so much,
Which we must ride dim ages round
Ere the hands (we dream) can touch,
We ride, we ride, before the morning
The secret roots of the sun to tread,
And suddenly
We are lifted of all we know
And hang from implacable boughs.

V. SACKVILLE-WEST

Wood-cut

When droning summer earth had slewed the shadows
Around the stable pivot of the sun,
Languid and lengthening across the meadows
The morn and eve in measure were as one.

V. SACKVILLE-WEST

Then sleepy rolled the earth to general slumber,
Shadowed yet shadowless within the dusk,
But still the sun-burnt hay-fields kept their umber,
And still the cornfields ripened in the husk,

While the young moon unsheathed her curving sabre
In the rinsed heaven of the greenish west,
And men maintained their sempiternal labour,
Taking no rest though earth herself took rest.

And while the last green light in heaven tarried
Behind the moving figures cut in black,
The last great loads of hay were safely carried
And heaped upon the shoulders of the stack.

Beyond the oasts, beyond the pricking gable,
Beyond the respite of the sleeping farm,
Beyond the stamping hoofs in cobbled stable,
Man stretched out day upon his tired arm;

Small man, but now in outline grown titanic
Heaving the trusses as the rick rose high;
The prongs of forks in silhouette satanic,
And rungs of ladders reared against the sky.

On the Lake

A candle lit in darkness of black waters,
A candle set in the drifting prow of a boat,
And every tree to itself a separate shape,
Now plumy, now an arch; tossed trees
Still and dishevelled; dishevelled with past growth,
Forgotten storms; left tufted, tortured, sky-rent,
Even now in stillness; stillness on the lake,
Black, reflections pooled, black mirror
Pooling a litten candle, taper of fire;
Pooling the sky, double transparency
Of sky in water, double elements,
Lying like lovers, light above, below:

V. SACKVILLE-WEST

Taking, from one another, light; a gleaming,
A glow reflected, fathoms deep, leagues high,
Two distances meeting at a film of surface
Thin as a membrane, sheet of surface, fine
Smooth steel; two separates, height and depth,
Able to touch, giving to one another
All their profundity, all their accidents,
—Changeable mood of clouds, permanent stars,—
Like thoughts in the mind hanging a long way off,
Revealed between lovers, friends. Peer in the water
Over the boat's edge; seek the sky's night-heart;
Are they near, are they far, those clouds, those stars
Given, reflected, pooled? are they so close
For a hand to clasp, to lift them, feel their shape,
Explore their reality, take a rough possession?
Oh no! too delicate, too shy for handling,
They tilt at a touch, quiver to other shapes,
Dance away, change, are lost, drowned, scared;
Hands break the mirror, speech's crudity
The surmise, the divining;
Such things so deeply held, so lightly held,
Subtile, imponderable, as stars in water
Or thoughts in another's thoughts.
Are they near, are they far, those stars, that knowledge?
Deep? shallow? solid? rare? The boat drifts on,
And the litten candle single in the prow,
The small, immediate candle in the prow
Burns brighter in the water than any star.

OSBERT SITWELL

To Charlotte Corday

Oh, Huntsman, when will the hunting stop;
And the spring begin;
And the first star-eyed blossoms
Sprinkle earth's dull skin,

And Man's sorrow be again
Of divine ordination,
Not this evil, dull fruit
Of Man's negation?

In all lands under wide skies found
Men turn down the light and burrow
Like moles in the ground;
Only bully, bore and busybody
In beetle-armour clad
Scuttle round and hurry round
With hearts that are glad.

Has no man the courage to forbid it,
Now that the hounds are so near;
Has all the world no man to rid it
Of the hearts that have caused this fear,
Of the icy hearts and the bragging voices,
So that all the world rejoices
In a day when death was dear?

December 1939

Giardino Pubblico

Petunias in mass formation,
An angry rose, a hard carnation,
Hot yellow grass, a yellow palm
Rising, giraffe-like, into calm
—All these glare hotly in the sun.
Behind are woods, where shadows run
Like water through the dripping shade
That leaf and laughing wind have made.
Here silence, like a silver bird,
Pecks at the peach-ripe heat . . . We heard
Townward, the voices, glazed with starch,
Of tourists on belated march

From church to church, to praise by rule
The beauties of the Tuscan School,
Clanging of trams, a hidden flute,
Sharp as the taste of unripe fruit;
Street organs join with tolling bell
To threaten us with both Heaven and Hell;
But through all taps a nearing sound
As of stage horses pawing ground.
Then like a whale, confined in cage,
(In grandeur of a borrowed carriage)
The old Marchesa swims in sight
In tinkling jet that braves the light,
Making the sun hit out each tone
As if it played the xylophone,
'Till she seems like a rainbow, where
She swells and, whale-like, spouts the air.

·   ·   ·   ·   ·   ·

In passing, she imposed her will
Upon all things both live and still;
Lovers hid quickly—none withstood
That awful glance of widowhood;
Each child, each tree, the shrilling heat
Became encased in glacial jet;
The very songbird in the air
Was now a scarecrow dangling there,
While, if you turned to stare, you knew
The punishment Lot's wife went through.

·   ·   ·   ·   ·   ·

Her crystal cage moves on. Stagnation
Thaws once again to animation.
Gladly the world receives reprieve
Till six o'clock tomorrow eve,
When punctual as the sun, she'll drive
Life out of everything alive,
Then in gigantic glory, fade
Sunward through the western glade. . . .

OSBERT SITWELL

Lament for Richard Rolston

Where do you sing your hymns,
  Savouring the oily tunes upon your tongue,
Send them rolling out from your huge lung;
Where now in the early spring do you paint the rockery white;
In what sensual heaven for sailors
Have you taken up your abode,
You who were so robustly alive, late on the road?

You lived in your humour orotund and in a world of wonder,
Watching the sky, catching the mutter of thunder,
Tasting the wine, till it raced in your veins like a whale's,
Watching the skid on the window of rain as it flails
On the grass, thinking of the sea always, of the ship plunging.

RICHARD CHURCH

Nocturne

See how the dying west puts forth her song,
Soft stars for requiem, hung bosom-low,
Riding like sorrow as day breathes her last
With deep-drawn sigh. The wintry Hunter long,
Long since has vanished in his frosty race,
Calling his Dog into the south below,
Striding to fresh eternities. The sky
Holds now but peaceful fires, beacons of grace,
Lanterns for mating-lips to meet, and eyes
To gleam beneath, troubled with prophecies
And births foretold. The rustling creepers fold
Their ghostly fingers, cold with clasping green,
Round all things bared by winter misery.
The cuckoo lingers in the woodland deeps
Long after thrushes' silence, long after mellow
Slow, pouring, yellow-mouthed notes

Have died on the ousel's throat, leaving the air
Tumultuous. Hark, oh rapt listeners!
Strange hands pluck at the forest branches, strains
Waft upward, legendary notes, and lore
Holding such harmony that beauty floats
Half unheard upon it from the seared
Heart of the nightingale.
                              Ah! could they hear
Those sleeping innocents, could they draw near
Even in sleep, what would their childhood thought
Construe from this slow agony, so fraught
With centuries of brooding? But no! deep,
Deep they lie, so late the night has grown,
Safe under eaves and attic, all their dreams
Garnered in other worlds behind the close
Firm-bolted eyelids; and the daylight mirth
With all its fleetness stalled behind the tread
Of slumber-pacing lips, that count the hours
In vital blood-pulse, as the souls within
Ride up and fall like ships upon the tide.

The tide! The ebb, the flow of life. It comes
Almost with visible waves upon the night,
This earth but jetsam, and our dreams but wrack,
Tumbling our music over, and our old
Familiar leaf and feather, voice and thought.
Hark! you mothers, and you expectant brides,
Hear in yourselves the lapping waves creep up,
Carrying others to the ancient sides
And shores of isled mortality, time-wrought
And garlanded with spring. It is through you
That beauty lives, you make the midnight sing!

Waiting for News

Waiting for news! What news?
News from the darkness, how the seed
Should bestir itself in greed,

RICHARD CHURCH

Clutch, consume, and break the soil,
Then, with no moment more to lose,
Stretch out, stretch up, and from that toil
With leafy voices claim to be
King in the forest dynasty.

Waiting for news! What news?
News from the unknown, where the worm
Listens in its earthy form,
And hungry for what all worms lack,
Tunnels upward and pursues
The would-be monarch, drags him back,
Digests, then leaves for further grace,
A spiral in his royal place.

Waiting for news! What news?
News from the light, the known, where man
Comes, as only human can,
To dig with sharp and shining spade
How he likes, and where he choose
In the wormy forest glade.
Waiting for news of mankind's will.
Waiting for news—but waiting still!

ROBERT NICHOLS

By the Wood

How still the day is, and the air how bright!
A thrush sings and is silent in the wood;
The hillside sleeps dizzy with heat and light;
A rhythmic murmur fills the quietude;
A woodpecker prolongs his leisured flight,
Rising and falling on the solitude.

But there are those who far from yon wood lie,
Buried within the trench where all were found;
A weight of mould oppresses every eye;
Within that cabin close their limbs are bound,
And there they rot amid the long profound,
Disastrous silence of grey earth and sky.

Those also rested where now rests but one,
Who scarce can lift his panged and heavy head,
Who drinks in grief the hot light of the sun,
Whose eyes watch dully the green branches spread
Who feels his currents ever slowlier run,
Whose lips repeat a silent ". . . Dead! all dead!"

O Youth, to come, shall drink air warm and bright,
Shall hear the bird cry in the sunny wood,
All my Young England fell to-day in fight;
That bird, that wood was ransomed by our blood!
I pray you when the drum rolls let your mood
Be worthy of our deaths and your delight.

I Love a Flower

I love a flower which has no lover,
    The yellow sea-poppy is its name;
Spined leaves its glaucous green stem cover,
    Its flower is a yellow fitful flame.

Stung by the spray which leaps the shingle,
    Torn by the winds that scour the beach,
Its roots with the salt sea-wrack mingle,
    Its leaves among the bleached stones bleach.

Its desperate growth but few remember,
    None misses it when it has died—
Scorched by the sun to a scant ember
    Or wholly ravaged by the tide.

Yet I elect this weed to cherish,
  Nor any other would desire
Than this, which must so shortly perish
  Tortured by sea-foam or sky-fire.

Above this flower we two once bended,
  Drawn to it by a subtle spell,
On whom the fire of heaven descended,
  Over whom the wave arose from hell.

Frantic, she snatched the ragged blossom,
  Kissed it, then, with a wild fierce kiss,
Thrust spine and flame into her bosom,
  Crying, "The flower! our love is this!"

The grey waves crash. The wind whirls over.
  The flower is withered from the beach,
Whose waves divide the loved and lover,
  Whose wind blows louder than their speech.

WILFRED OWEN

Futility

Move him into the sun—
Gently its touch awoke him once,
At home, whispering of fields unsown.
Always it woke him, even in France,
Until this morning and this snow.
If anything might rouse him now
The kind old sun will know.

Think how it wakes the seeds,—
Woke, once, the clays of a cold star.
Are limbs, so dear-achieved, are sides,
Full-nerved—still warm—too hard to stir?
Was it for this the clay grew tall?
—O what made fatuous sunbeams toil
To break earth's sleep at all?

Insensibility

I

Happy are men who yet before they are killed
Can let their veins run cold.
Whom no compassion fleers
Or makes their feet
Sore on the alleys cobbled with their brothers.
The front line withers,
But they are troops who fade, not flowers
For poet's tearful fooling:
Men, gaps for filling:
Losses who might have fought
Longer; but no one bothers.

II

And some cease feeling
Even themselves or for themselves.
Dullness best solves
The tease and doubt of shelling,
And Chance's strange arithmetic
Comes simpler than the reckoning of their shilling.
They keep no check on armies' decimation.

III

Happy are these who lose imagination:
They have enough to carry with ammunition.
Their spirit drags no pack,
Their old wounds save with cold can not more ache.
Having seen all things red,
Their eyes are rid
Of the hurt of the colour of blood for ever.
And terror's first constriction over,
Their hearts remain small-drawn.
Their senses in some scorching cautery of battle
Now long since ironed,
Can laugh among the dying, unconcerned.

IV

Happy the soldier home, with not a notion
How somewhere, every dawn, some men attack,
And many sighs are drained.
Happy the lad whose mind was never trained:
His days are worth forgetting more than not.
He sings along the march
Which we march taciturn, because of dusk,
The long, forlorn, relentless trend
From larger day to huger night.

V

We wise, who with a thought besmirch
Blood over all our soul,
How should we see our task
But through his blunt and lashless eyes?
Alive, he is not vital overmuch;
Dying, not mortal overmuch;
Nor sad, nor proud,
Nor curious at all.
He cannot tell
Old men's placidity from his.

VI

But cursed are dullards whom no cannon stuns,
That they should be as stones;
Wretched are they, and mean
With paucity that never was simplicity.
By choice they made themselves immune
To pity and whatever moans in man
Before the last sea and the hapless stars;
Whatever mourns when many leave these shores;
Whatever shares
The eternal reciprocity of tears.

WILFRED OWEN

Strange Meeting

It seemed that out of battle I escaped
Down some profound dull tunnel, long since scooped
Through granites which titanic wars had groined.
Yet also there encumbered sleepers groaned,
Too fast in thought or death to be bestirred.
Then, as I probed them, one sprang up, and stared
With piteous recognition in fixed eyes,
Lifting distressful hands as if to bless.
And by his smile, I knew that sullen hall,
By his dead smile I knew we stood in Hell.
With a thousand pains that vision's face was grained;
Yet no blood reached there from the upper ground,
And no guns thumped, or down the flues made moan.
"Strange friend," I said, "here is no cause to mourn."
"None," said the other, "save the undone years,
The hopelessness. Whatever hope is yours,
Was my life also; I went hunting wild
After the wildest beauty in the world,
Which lies not calm in eyes, or braided hair,
But mocks the steady running of the hour,
And if it grieves, grieves richlier than here.
For by my glee might many men have laughed,
And of my weeping something had been left,
Which must die now. I mean the truth untold,
The pity of war, the pity war distilled.
Now men will go content with what we spoiled.
Or, discontent, boil bloody, and be spilled.
They will be swift with swiftness of the tigress,
None will break ranks, though nations trek from progress.
Courage was mine, and I had mystery,
Wisdom was mine, and I had mastery;
To miss the march of this retreating world
Into vain citadels that are not walled.
Then, when much blood had clogged their chariot-wheels
I would go up and wash them from sweet wells,
Even with truths that lie too deep for taint.

I would have poured my spirit without stint
But not through wounds; not on the cess of war.
Foreheads of men have bled where no wounds were.
I am the enemy you killed, my friend.
I knew you in this dark; for so you frowned
Yesterday through me as you jabbed and killed.
I parried; but my hands were loath and cold.
Let us sleep now. . . ."

Apologia Pro Poemate Meo

I, too, saw God through mud,—
    The mud that cracked on cheeks when wretches smiled.
    War brought more glory to their eyes than blood,
    And gave their laughs more glee than shakes a child.

Merry it was to laugh there—
    Where death becomes absurd and life absurder.
    For power was on us as we slashed bones bare
    Not to feel sickness or remorse of murder.

I, too, have dropped off fear—
    Behind the barrage, dead as my platoon,
    And sailed my spirit surging, light and clear
    Past the entanglement where hopes lay strewn;

And witnessed exultation—
    Faces that used to curse me, scowl for scowl,
    Shine and lift up with passion of oblation,
    Seraphic for an hour; though they were foul.

I have made fellowships—
    Untold of happy lovers in old song.
    For love is not the binding of fair lips
    With the soft silk of eyes that look and long,

By Joy, whose ribbon slips,—
    But wound with war's hard wire whose stakes are strong;

WILFRED OWEN

Bound with the bandage of the arm that drips;
Knit in the webbing of the rifle-thong.

I have perceived much beauty
In the hoarse oaths that kept our courage straight;
Heard music in the silentness of duty;
Found peace where shell-storms spouted reddest spate.

Nevertheless, except you share
With them in hell the sorrowful dark of hell,
Whose world is but the trembling of a flare,
And heaven but as the highway for a shell,

You shall not hear their mirth:
You shall not come to think them well content
By any jest of mine. These men are worth
Your tears. You are not worth their merriment.

November 1917

HERBERT READ

A Song for the Spanish Anarchists

The golden lemon is not made
  but grows on a green tree:
A strong man and his crystal eyes
  is a man born free.

The oxen pass under the yoke
  and the blind are led at will:
But a man born free has a path of his own
  and a house on the hill.

And men are men who till the land
  and women are women who weave:
Fifty men own the lemon grove
  and no man is a slave.

HERBERT READ

To a Conscript of 1940

Qui n'a pas une fois désespéré de l'honneur, ne sera jamais un héros.
GEORGES BERNANOS

A soldier passed me in the freshly-fallen snow,
His footsteps muffled, his face unearthly grey;
And my heart gave a sudden leap
As I gazed on a ghost of five-and-twenty years ago.

I shouted Halt! and my voice had the old accustom'd ring
And he obeyed it as it was obeyed
In the shrouded days when I too was one
Of an army of young men marching

Into the unknown. He turned towards me and I said:
"I am one of those who went before you
Five-and-twenty years ago: one of the many who never returned,
Of the many who returned and yet were dead.

We went where you are going, into the rain and the mud;
We fought as you will fight
With death and darkness and despair;
We gave what you will give—our brains and our blood.

We think we gave in vain. The world was not renewed.
There was hope in the homestead and anger in the streets
But the old world was restored and we returned
To the dreary field and workshop and the immemorial feud

Of rich and poor. Our victory was our defeat.
Power was retained where power had been misused
And youth was left to sweep away
The ashes that the fires had strewn beneath our feet.

But one thing we learned: there is no glory in the deed
Until the soldier wears a badge of tarnish'd braid;
There are heroes who have heard the rally and have seen
The glitter of a garland round their head.

Theirs is the hollow victory. They are deceived.
But you, my brother and my ghost, if you can go
Knowing that there is no reward, no certain use
In all your sacrifice, then honour is reprieved.

To fight without hope is to fight with grace,
The self reconstructed, the false heart repaired."
Then I turned with a smile, and he answered my salute
As he stood against the fretted hedge, which was like white
    lace.

The Sorrow of Unicume

Fresh in the flush light gleam
the slape new furrows:
ride the clean horizon rib
lithe Unicume and his roan team.

Man moulded with Earth—
like day uprisen:
his whistling mingles
with the throstle's this even.

Inward from furtive woods
the stretched light stains:
end-toil star now broods
deeming resthaven due.

Unyoked the roan team
garthward he leads:
hooves beat to harness clink;
the swollen sun bleeds.

2.

When alone, Unicume
seeks his darkening dale.
Yon my white garden-rail—
Heart's tomb within!

HERBERT READ

He lifts latch to the quiet room
where yet it seems she breathes:
he kneels to take her stark hands
in caress mute with the gloom.

"*Draw the casement, let me see*
last light without."
Ah, fierce the white, white stars to hurt,
their beauty a wild shout.

Retch of flower-scent, lush decay
Among time-burdened shrubs.
And near and shallowly buried lay
Love once enflesh'd, now fled.

3.

Harsh my heart is,
scalded with grief:
my life a limp
worm-eaten leaf.

White flower unfeeling,
you star the mould:
evolvèd calmness,
my heart enfold.

LILIAN BOWES LYON

A Shepherd's Coat

I woke from death and dreaming.
His absence be the child I carry,
All days, and all years.
Eternally and this night he will deliver me.
Come peace. For he is coming.

Time tells a marginal story;
Dilutes with midsummer that less than leaf
A mute heart, light heart, blown along the pavement;
Then mortally wintry, sears
The implicit glade—oh universe enough!
Orchard in bloom bereaved beyond bereavement.
Yet peace! For now it is gloaming,
Simple and provident, folding the numbered lambs.

No spatial streams, no tears
Can melt the insensate piety of grief.
Adore instead the untold event still happening;
That miracle be the child I carry,
All days, and all years.
Come other south, come wise and holier thaws,
Enlarge me to inhale so ample a breath;
Come peace for he is coming.
Between the lily in bud and the lily opening
Love is, and love redeems.
Come haven, come your hush, horizoning arms.

I shall not want, I wake renewed by death,
A shepherd's coat drawn over me.

The Feather

A man and woman walking
   Up the rye hill
Had no breath for talking.
   The evening was still;

Only the wind in the rough grass
   Made a papery patter;
Like yesterday it was,
   Too spent a sigh to matter.

LILIAN BOWES LYON

Down fell a curlew's feather
    As they went on their way
(Who walked kindly together
    And had nothing to say),

So light, so soft, so strange,
    To have settled on her heart.
It was the breath of change,
    That breathed them apart.

The Stars Go By

A fox, in heaven's trap that gleams,
Bites his legs off in my dreams;
I shriek his pain, as torn I share
The white hurt of the wounded air.

The stars go by in glittering packs;
I'm still my heaven, still my fox;
Ten thousand suns revolve about
This burning Self that won't go out.

How dares the imprisoned soul find fault
With holy Creation's crystal vault?
Let worlds mark time and stars go by;
In terrible love with truth I lie.

Towers a light to lift man up;
My heaven is drained in a brilliant drop;
Salt on the tongue I feel the smart
Of the blood of the fox that gnaws my heart.

ROBERT GRAVES

The Cool Web

Children are dumb to say how hot the day is,
How hot the scent is of the summer rose,
How dreadful the black wastes of evening sky,
How dreadful the tall soldiers drumming by.

But we have speech to chill the angry day,
And speech, to dull the rose's cruel scent.
We spell away the overhanging night,
We spell away the soldiers and the fright.

There's a cool web of language winds us in,
Retreat from too much joy or too much fear:
We grow sea-green at last and coldly die
In brininess and volubility.

But if we let our tongues lose self-possession,
Throwing off language and its watery clasp
Before our death, instead of when death comes,
Facing the wide glare of the children's day,
Facing the rose, the dark sky and the drums,
We shall go mad no doubt and die that way.

Lost Love

His eyes are quickened so with grief,
He can watch a grass or leaf
Every instant grow; he can
Clearly through a flint wall see,
Or watch the startled spirit flee
From the throat of a dead man.
  Across two counties he can hear
And catch your words before you speak.
The woodlouse or the maggot's weak
Clamour rings in his sad ear,
And noise so slight it would surpass
Credence—drinking sound of grass,
Worm talk, clashing jaws of moth
Chumbling holes in cloth;
The groan of ants who undertake
Gigantic loads for honour's sake
(Their sinews creak, their breath comes thin);
Whir of spiders when they spin,
And minute whispering, mumbling, sighs
Of idle grubs and flies.

This man is quickened so with grief,
He wanders god-like or like thief
Inside and out, below, above,
Without relief seeking lost love.

1805

At Viscount Nelson's lavish funeral,
    While the mob milled and yelled about St. Paul's,
A General chatted with an Admiral:

"One of your colleagues, Sir, remarked today
    That Nelson's *exit*, though to be lamented,
Falls not inopportunely, in its way."

"He was a thorn in our flesh," came the reply—
    "The most bird-witted, unaccountable,
Odd little runt that ever I did spy.

"One arm, one peeper, vain as Pretty Poll,
    A meddler, too, in foreign politics
And gave his heart in pawn to a plain moll.

"He would dare lecture us Sea Lords, and then
    Would treat his ratings as though men of honour
And play at leap-frog with his midshipmen!

"We tried to box him down, but up he popped,
    And when he'd banged Napoleon at the Nile
Became too much the hero to be dropped.

"You've heard that Copenhagen 'blind eye' story?
    We'd tied him to Nurse Parker's apron-strings—
By G-d, he snipped them through and snatched the glory!"

"Yet," cried the General, "six-and-twenty sail
    Captured or sunk by him off Tráfalgár—
That writes a handsome *finis* to the tale."

"Handsome enough. The seas are England's now.
  That fellow's foibles need no longer plague us.
He died most creditably, I'll allow."

"And, Sir, the secret of his victories?"
  "By his unServicelike, familiar ways, Sir,
He made the whole Fleet love him, damn his eyes!"

The Presence

Why say "death"? Death is neither harsh nor kind:
Other pleasures or pains could hold the mind
If she were dead. For dead is gone indeed,
Lost beyond recovery or need,
Discarded, ended, rotted underground—
Of whom no personal feature could be found
To stand out from the soft blur evenly spread·
On memory, if she were truly dead.

But living still, barred from accustomed use
Of body and dress and motion, with profuse
Reproaches (since this anguish of her grew
Do I still love her as I swear I do?)
She fills the house and garden terribly
With her bewilderment, accusing me,
Till every stone and flower, table and book,
Cries out her name, pierces me with her look,
"You are deaf, listen!
You are blind, see!"
              How deaf or blind,
When horror of the grave maddens the mind
With those same pangs that lately choked her breath,
Altered her substance, and made sport of death?

Ulysses

To the much-tossed Ulysses, never done
  With woman whether gowned as wife or whore,
Penelope and Circe seemed as one:

She like a whore made his lewd fancies run,
And wifely she a hero to him bore.

Their counter-changings terrified his way:
  They were the clashing rocks, Symplegades,
Scylla and Charybdis too were they;
Now they were storms frosting the sea with spray
  And now the lotus island's drunken ease.

They multiplied into the Sirens' throng,
  Forewarned by fear of whom he stood bound fast
Hand and foot helpless to the vessel's mast,
Yet would not stop his ears: daring their song
  He groaned and sweated till that shore was past.

One, two and many: flesh had made him blind,
  Flesh had one pleasure only in the act,
Flesh set one purpose only in the mind—
Triumph of flesh and afterwards to find
  Still those same terrors wherewith flesh was racked.

His wiles were witty and his fame far known,
Every king's daughter sought him for her own,
  Yet he was nothing to be won or lost.
  All lands to him were Ithaca: love tossed
He loathed the fraud, yet would not bed alone.

The Foreboding

Looking by chance in at the open window
  I saw my own self seated in his chair
With gaze abstracted, furrowed forehead,
  Unkempt hair.

I thought that I had suddenly come to die,
  That to a cold corpse this was my farewell,
Until the pen moved slowly upon paper
  And tears fell.

ROBERT GRAVES

He had written a name, yours, in printed letters:
  One word on which bemusedly to pore—
No protest, no desire, your naked name,
  Nothing more.

Would it be tomorrow, would it be next year?
  But the vision was not false, this much I knew;
And I turned angrily from the open window
  Aghast at you.

Why never a warning, either by speech or look,
  That the love you cruelly gave me could not last?
Already it was too late: the bait swallowed,
  The hook fast.

EDMUND BLUNDEN

Behind the Line

Treasure not so the forlorn days
When dun clouds flooded the naked plains
  With foul remorseless rains;
  Tread not those memory ways
Where by the dripping alien farms,
Starved orchards with their shrivelled arms,
The bitter mouldering wind would whine
At the brisk mules clattering towards the Line.

Remember not with so sharp skill
Each chasm in the clouds that strange with fire
  Lit pyramid-fosse and spire
  Miles on miles from our hill;
In the magic glass, aye, then their lure
Like heaven's houses gleaming pure
Might soothe the long-imprisoned sight
And put the double storm to flight.

Enact not you so like a wheel
The round of evenings in sandbagged rooms
　　Where candles flicked the glooms;
　　The jests old time could steal
From ugly destiny, on whose brink
The poor fools grappled fear with drink,
And snubbed the hungry raving guns
With endless tunes on gramophones.

About you spreads the world anew,
The old fields all for your sense rejoice,
　　Music has found her ancient voice,
　　From the hills there's heaven on earth to view;
And kindly Mirth will raise his glass
With you to bid dull Care go pass—
And still you wander muttering on
Over the shades of shadows gone.

Forefathers

　　Here they went with smock and crook,
　　　　Toiled in the sun, lolled in the shade,
　　Here they mudded out the brook
　　　　And here their hatchet cleared the glade:
　　Harvest-supper woke their wit,
　　Huntsman's moon their wooings lit.

　　From this church they led their brides,
　　　　From this church themselves were led
　　Shoulder-high; on these waysides
　　　　Sat to take their beer and bread.
　　Names are gone—what men they were
　　These their cottages declare.

　　Names are vanished, save the few
　　　　In the old brown Bible scrawled;
　　These were men of pith and thew,
　　　　Whom the city never called;
　　Scarce could read or hold a quill,
　　Built the barn, the forge, the mill.

On the green they watched their sons
  Playing till too dark to see,
As their fathers watched them once,
  As my father once watched me;
While the bat and beetle flew
On the warm air webbed with dew.

Unrecorded, unrenowned,
  Men from whom my ways begin,
Here I know you by your ground
  But I know you not within—
There is silence, there survives
Not a moment of your lives.

Like the bee that now is blown
  Honey-heavy on my hand,
From his toppling tansy-throne
  In the green tempestuous land,—
I'm in clover now, nor know
Who made honey long ago.

The Sunlit Vale

I saw the sunlit vale, and the pastoral fairy-tale;
The sweet and bitter scent of the may drifted by;
And never have I seen such a bright bewildering green,
  But it looked like a lie,
  Like a kindly meant lie.

When gods are in dispute, one a Sidney, one a brute,
It would seem that human sense might not know, might not
    spy;
But though nature smile and feign where foul play has stabbed
    and slain,
  There's a witness, an eye,
  Nor will charms blind that eye.

EDMUND BLUNDEN

Nymph of the upland song and the sparkling leafage young,
For your merciful desire with these charms to beguile,
For ever be adored; muses yield you rich reward;
   But you fail, though you smile—
   That other does not smile.

What is Winter?

   The haze upon the meadow
     Denies the dying year
For the sun's within it, something bridal
     Is more than dreaming here.
There is no end, no severance,
No moment of deliverance,
     No quietus made,
Though quiet abounds and deliverance moves
     In that sunny shade.

     What is winter? a word,
     A figure, a clever guess.
That time-word does not answer to
     This drowsy wakefulness.
The secret stream scorns interval
Though the calendar shouts one from the wall;
     The spirit has no last days;
And death is no more dead than this
     Flower-haunted haze.

RUTH PITTER

Time's Fool

Time's fool, but not heaven's: yet hope not for any return.
The rabbit-eaten dry branch and the halfpenny candle
Are lost with the other treasure: the sooty kettle
Thrown away, become redbreast's home in the hedge, where the
   nettle
Shoots up, and bad bindweed wreathes rust-fretted handle.
Under that broken thing no more shall the dry branch burn.

Poor comfort all comfort: once what the mouse had spared
Was enough, was delight, there where the heart was at home;
The hard cankered apple holed by the wasp and the bird,
The damp bed, with the beetle's tap in the headboard heard,
The dim bit of mirror, three inches of comb:
Dear enough, when with youth and with fancy shared.

I knew that the roots were creeping under the floor,
That the toad was safe in his hole, the poor cat by the fire,
The starling snug in the roof, each slept in his place:
The lily in splendour, the vine in her grace,
The fox in the forest, all had their desire,
As then I had mine, in the place that was happy and poor.

SACHEVERELL SITWELL

Derbyshire Bluebells

The wood is one blue flame of love,
It trembles with the thrush and dove;
Who is this honey beacon for,
That burns this once, then never more?
What lutes hide in the young green leaves?
Who sorrows here when no one grieves?

The misty spaces in the boughs,
No shouts will fill, no stone will rouse,
If at those panes we beat in vain
Why hope to quench that fire with rain?
Why beat the bluebells down to find
How fire and honey are combined?

There is no space for foot to tread
Unless you bruise the flower head,
No corner where you cannot hear
The dove's long croon, the thrush sing near,
Like bells out of the trees' tall spires
These songs above the bluebell fires.

This fire of little bells, sweet eyes,
Climbs into the dove throat skies,
It shines, as here, at Bolsover
And to that Venus is a lover;
It burns in all the haunted woods
And marries with the castle's moods.

Stone Venus on her fountain ledge,
Can see above the hornbeam hedge
The only fire that climbs to her,
For sun and moon shine down on her;
And these can only reach the brim,
If they were wingèd seraphim.

Not bluebells, but bright angels' plumes,
Then burning where the sun illumes
This sharp blue fire would be her lover
And she would need no other cover,
With thrush and dove for beating heart
And bluebells hiding every part.

The casement in the castle wall
Hears the Venus fountain call,
The lutes, long dead, ring out again
And beauty like a gentle rain
Shines on each thing that has died,
Made live now with the bluebell tide.

This world of few days and few nights,
These fancies that this blue invites,
Seeks the dark, the light it shuns,
And haunts the clouded mullions,
This honey music of the spring
It winnows with the pigeon's wing.

So where deep peace should be, and quiet,
These ghosts fill with the lute's loud riot,

They hold a noisy tournament
Half-hidden in the bluebell's scent,
And Venus is but dimly seen
For lute strings and the flowers' blue screen.

We leave the mist for Renishaw
And tall elms where the rooks do caw;
But when I walk our silent woods,
Now broken with the dove's sad moods,
Not Venus, nor her lutes, I miss,
Nor find our bluebells honeyless.

Outside Dunsandle

What a liar
Was the tinker woman whom we met
Under the long stone wall!
But what a creature of mystery
With her tousled terrible child,
Eating bread,
And her veiled eyes.

She told us the wrong way to go,
Only for a few coppers,
Knowing we should come back again.
She watched, while the boy
With frayed sleeves and groundsel hair
Munched away.

She would have sent us over the edge
    of the world
For a few pennies,
Far away there out in the west.
I see her in the long rags of rain
Gathering wet sticks
For the turf fire,
Waiting for lost travellers to come by.

EDGELL RICKWORD

The Cascade

Lovers may find similitudes
to the sweet babbling girlish noise,
in the inhuman crystal voice
that calls from mountain solitudes;

as that's but movement overlaid
with water, a faint shining thought,
spirit is to music wrought
in the swift passion of a maid.

It is her body sings so clear,
chanting in the woods of night,
on Earth's dark precipice a white
Prometheus, bound like water here;

the eager Joys toward their task
from dusky veins beat up in flocks,
but still her curious patience mocks
the consummation lovers ask.

Lying on ferns she seems to wear
(the silver tissue of the skin
radiant from the fire within)
light as her weed and shade for hair;

rapt in communion so intense
the nicer senses fail and she,
sweet Phoenix, burns on Pain's rich tree
in praise and prayer and frankincense.

The iron beaks that seek her flesh
vex more her lovers' anxious minds,
in whose dim glades each hunter finds
his own torn spirit in his mesh.

EDGELL RICKWORD

Rimbaud in Africa

In the character of the damned conjurer

Through my small town I roamed, a taunting ghost
out of a world like rock and wind to yours,
and counted friends and honour nothing lost
to feed the inner pride that burned my hours.

Faustus, whom your academy once crowned,
spent midnight oil on ill-spelt smutty books;
your approbation's dirty insult drowned
in comradeship with idiots and crooks.

Beauty is epicene, whipped slave to show,
yet Helen swan-like glided to his bed,
whom he put scornfully away as though
he sought no pleasure in the life he led.

Such hot disdain scorched desert solitude
around him, where he practised magic art;
from elemental soul sublimed a crude
companion who would share no human heart;

all the devotion of his spirit yearned
on this frail vessel and refined its clay
till with slow eyes it answered him and turned
his pride to wings and went its lonely way.

Now Faustus in the desert trades for gold,
nations acknowledge his peculiar spell;
an utter silence feeds the pride grown old;
respect is mockery and sharpens hell.

ROY CAMPBELL

The Sisters

After hot loveless nights, when cold winds stream
Sprinkling the frost and dew, before the light,
Bored with the foolish things that girls must dream
Because their beds are empty of delight,

Two sisters rise and strip. Out from the night
Their horses run to their low-whistled pleas—
Vast phantom shapes with eyeballs rolling white
That sneeze a fiery steam about their knees:

Through the crisp manes their stealthy prowling hands,
Stronger than curbs, in slow caresses rove,
They gallop down across the milk-white sands
And wade far out into the sleeping cove:

The frost stings sweetly with a burning kiss
As intimate as love, as cold as death:
Their lips, whereon delicious tremors hiss,
Fume with the ghostly pollen of their breath.

Far out on the grey silence of the flood
They watch the dawn in smouldering gyres expand
Beyond them: and the day burns through their blood
Like a white candle through a shuttered hand.

Buffel's Kop

(Olive Schreiner's Grave)

In after times when strength or courage fail,
May I recall this lonely hour: the gloom
Moving one way: all heaven in the gale
Roaring: and high above the insulted tomb
An eagle anchored on full spread of sail
That from its wings let fall a silver plume.

ROY CAMPBELL

The Zulu Girl

When in the sun the hot red acres smoulder,
Down where the sweating gang its labour plies,
A girl flings down her hoe, and from her shoulder
Unslings her child tormented by the flies.

She takes him to a ring of shadow pooled
By thorn-trees: purpled with the blood of ticks,
While her sharp nails, in slow caresses ruled,
Prowl through his hair with sharp electric clicks,

His sleepy mouth, plugged by the heavy nipple,
Tugs like a puppy, grunting as he feeds:
Through his frail nerves her own deep languors ripple
Like a broad river sighing through its reeds.

Yet in that drowsy stream his flesh imbibes
An old unquenched unsmotherable heat—
The curbed ferocity of beaten tribes,
The sullen dignity of their defeat.

Her body looms above him like a hill
Within whose shade a village lies at rest,
Or the first cloud so terrible and still
That bears the coming harvest in its breast.

On Some South African Novelists

You praise the firm restraint with which they write,
I'm with you there, of course:
They use the snaffle and the curb all right,
But where's the bloody horse?

MICHAEL ROBERTS

The Caves

This is the cave of which I spoke,
These are the blackened stones, and these
Our footprints, seven lives ago.

Darkness was in the cave like shifting smoke,
Stalagmites grew like equatorial trees,
There was a pool, quite black and silent, seven lives ago.

Here such a one turned back, and there
Another stumbled and his nerve gave out;
Men have escaped blindly, they know not how.

Our candles gutter in the mouldering air,
Here the rock fell, beyond a doubt,
There was no light in those days, and there is none now.

Water drips from the roof, and the caves narrow,
Galleries lead downward to the unknown dark;
This was the point we reached, the farthest known.

Here someone in the debris found an arrow,
Men have been here before, and left their mark
Scratched on the limestone wall with splintered bone.

Here the dark word was said for memory's sake,
And lost, here on the cold sand, to the puzzled brow.

This was the farthest point, the fabled lake:
These were our footprints, seven lives ago.

The Green Lake

Eloquent are the hills: their power speaks
In ice, rock and falling stone;
The voices of croziered fern, wood-sorrel, gentian, edelweiss,
Lead upward to the summit or the high col.

MICHAEL ROBERTS

The mountain lake mirrors the hills, and the white clouds
Move in a blue depth, the hut stands empty:
No one appears all day, nothing disturbs
The symphony of ice and yellow rock and the blue shadow.

And at dusk the familiar sequence: the light
Lingering on the peak; and near the horizon
Apricot-coloured skies, then purple; and the first stars;
An hour of bustle in the hut, and then silence.

Only at two in the morning men stir in the bunks,
Look out of the windows, put on their boots,
Exchange a word with the guardian, curse the cold,
And move with a force beyond their own to the high peaks.

Be still for once. Do not sing,
Let the blood beat its symphony unanswered;
Remain here by the lake for a whole day
With the sky clear and the rocks asking to be climbed.

There is music in movement, in the song, the dance,
The swing of the accordion in the crowded hut,
The swing of the axe in the icefall; but be still.
Listen. There is another voice that speaks.

A. S. J. TESSIMOND

The Children Look at the Parents

We being so hidden from those who
Have quietly borne and fed us,
How can we answer civilly
Their innocent invitations?

How can we say "we see you
As but-for-God's-grace-ourselves, as
Our caricatures (we yours), with
Time's telescope between us"?

How can we say "you presumed on
The accident of kinship,
Assumed our friendship coatlike,
Not as a badge one fights for"?

How say "and you remembered
The sins of our outlived selves and
Your own forgiveness, buried
The hatchet to slow music;

Shared money but not your secrets;
Will leave as your final legacy
A box double-locked by the spider
Packed with your unsolved problems"?

How say all this without capitals,
Italics, anger or pathos,
To those who have seen from the womb come
Enemies? How not say it?

One Almost Might

Wouldn't you say,
Wouldn't you say: one day,
With a little more time or a little more patience, one
   might
Disentangle for separate, deliberate, slow delight
One of the moment's hundred strands, unfray
Beginnings from endings, this from that, survey
Say a square inch of the ground one stands on, touch
Part of oneself or a leaf or a sound (not clutch
Or cuff or bruise but touch with finger-tip, ear-
Tip, eye-tip, creeping near yet not too near);
Might take up life and lay it on one's palm
And, encircling it in closeness, warmth and calm,
Let it lie still, then stir smooth-softly, and
Tendril by tendril unfold, there on one's hand. . . .

One might examine eternity's cross-section
For a second, with slightly more patience, more time
   for reflection?

The British

We are a people living in shells and moving
Crablike; reticent, awkward, deeply suspicious;
Watching the world from a corner of half-closed eyelids,
Afraid lest someone show that he hates or loves us,
Afraid lest someone weep in the railway train.

We are coiled and clenched like a foetus clad in armour.
We hold our hearts for fear they fly like eagles.
We grasp our tongues for fear they cry like trumpets.
We listen to our own footsteps. We look both ways
Before we cross the silent empty road.

We are a people easily made uneasy,
Especially wary of praise, of passion, of scarlet
Cloaks, of gesturing hands, of the smiling stranger
In the alien hat who talks to all, or the other
In the unfamiliar coat who talks to none.

We are afraid of too-cold thought or too-hot
Blood, of the opening of long-shut shafts or cupboards
Of light in caves, of X-rays, probes, unclothing
Of emotion, intolerable revelation
Of lust in the light, of love in the palm of the hand.

We are afraid of, one day on a sunny morning,
Meeting ourselves or another without the usual
Outer sheath, the comfortable conversation,
And saying all, all, all we did not mean to,
All, all, all we did not know we meant.

WILLIAM PLOMER

Archaic Apollo

Dredged in a net the slender god
Lies on deck and dries in the sun,
His head set proudly on his neck
Like a runner's whose race is won.

On his breast the Aegean lay
While the whole of history was made;
That long caress could not warm the flesh
Nor the antique smile abrade.

He is as he was, inert, alert,
The one hand open, the other lightly shut,
His nostrils clean as holes in a flute,
The nipples and navel delicately cut.

The formal eyes are calm and sly,
Of knowledge and joy a perfect token—
The world being caught in the net of the sky
No hush can drown a word once spoken.

The Prisoner

Every morning the prisoner hears
Calls to action and words of warning:
They fall not on deaf but indifferent ears.

Free speech, fresh air are denied him now,
Are not for one who is growing thin
Between four walls of Roman thickness.
From his cell he sees the meetings begin,
The vehement lock on the orator's brow
And the listeners warped by want and sickness.

His old wound throbs as old wounds will,
The summer morning makes his head feel light,
Painful the sunlight on the whitewashed sill,
Trembling he awaits the ever-fruitful night,
For then dreams many-formed appear
Teeming with truths that public lips ignore,
And naked figures struggle from the sea
Shipwrecked, to be clothed on shore,
And words no orator utters are said
Such as the wind through mouths of ivy forms
Or snails with silver write upon the dead
Bark of an ilex after April storms.

While flights of bombers streak his patch of sky,
While speakers rant and save the world with books,
While at the front the first battalions die,
Over the edge of thought itself he looks,
Tiptoe along a knife-edge he slowly travels,
Hears the storm roaring, the serpent hiss,
And the frail rope he hangs by, twisting, unravels,
As he steps so lightly over the abyss.

Tattooed

On his arms he wears
Diagrams he chose,
A snake inside a skull,
A dagger in a rose,

And the muscle playing
Under the skin
Makes the rose writhe
And the skull grin.

He is one who acts his dreams
And these emblems are a clue
To the wishes in his blood
And what they make him do,

These signs are truer
Than the wearer knows:
The blade vibrates
In the vulnerable rose,

Anthers bend, and carmine curly
Petals kiss the plunging steel,
Dusty with essential gold
Close in upon the thing they feel.

Moistly once in bony sockets
Eyeballs hinted at a soul,
In the death's head now a live head
Fills a different role;

Venomous resilience sliding
In the empty cave of thought,
Call it instinct ousting reason,
Or a reptile's indoor sport.

The flower's pangs, the snake exploring,
The skull, the violating knife,
Are the active and the passive
Aspects of his life,

Who is at home with death
More than he guesses;
The rose will die, and a skull
Gives back no caresses.

The Caledonian Market

A work-basket made of an old armadillo
    Lined with pink satin now rotten with age,
A novel entitled *The Ostracized Vicar*
    (A spider squashed flat on the title-page),

A faded album of nineteen-oh-seven
  Snapshots (now like very weak tea)
Showing high-collared knuts and girls expectant
  In big muslin hats at Bexhill-on-Sea,
A gasolier made of hand-beaten copper
  In the once modern style known as *art nouveau*,
An assegai, and a china slipper,
  And *What a Young Scoutmaster Ought to Know.* . . .

Who stood their umbrellas in elephants' feet?
  Who hung their hats on the horns of a moose?
Who crossed the ocean with amulets made
  To be hung round the neck of an ailing papoose?
Who paid her calls with a sandalwood card-case?
  From whose eighteen-inch waist hung that thin
    chatelaine?
Who smoked that meerschaum? Who won that medal?
  That extraordinary vase was evolved by what brain?
Who worked in wool the convolvulus bell-pull?
  Who smiled with those false teeth? Who wore that wig?
Who had that hair-tidy hung by her mirror?
  Whose was the scent-bottle shaped like a pig?

Where are the lads in their tight Norfolk jackets
  Who roistered in pubs that stayed open all day?
Where are the girls in their much tighter corsets
  And where are the figures they loved to display?
Where the old maids in their bric-à-brac settings
  With parlourmaids bringing them dinners and teas?
Where are their counterparts, idle old roués,
  Sodden old bachelors living at ease?
Where the big families, big with possessions,
  Their standards of living, their errors of taste?
Here are the soup-tureens—where is the ambience,
  Arrogance, confidence, hope without haste?

Laugh if you like at this monstrous detritus
  Of middle-class life in the liberal past,

The platypus stuffed, and the frightful epergne.
  You, who are now overtaxed and declassed,
Laugh while you can, for the time may come round
  When the rubbish *you* treasure will lie in this place—
Your wireless set (bust), your ridiculous hats,
  And the photographs of your period face.
Your best-selling novels, your "functional" chairs,
  Your primitive comforts and notions of style
Are just so much fodder for dealers in junk—
  Let us hope that they'll make your grandchildren smile.

STANLEY SNAITH

The Stack

Someone has left a stack
  Of thorn staves propped against the bank,
Still showing their primrose wounds, and trailed
  With leafage shrunk.

Though falling of neglect,
  Once they were packed and trussed for use,
To train young shoots perhaps, or burn
  For hearthside ease.

But no one comes this way:
  Grass blows in the bony prints of hooves,
And the brier drags across the path
  Among unraked leaves.

Spring has breathed her presence
  Down the lane, flowers are through, the spray
Leaps with alighting wings that bear
  Their morsel of wool or straw.

Who owns it now, the stack
  Shaved by the hook from living boughs—
Now that the marrying wrens are in
  Setting up house?

STANLEY SNAITH

Blue Ghosts

The climbing sun had drunk the shade
Out of the chalkpit; heat swayed
On stones, and the long-rainless soil
Stared, bright and naked as a skull.

Yet grass dug a bleak root to grow;
Thistle was swathed in rusting snow;
And clasped the chalk—spiked, witch-gnarled,
    bent—
A furze bush dissolute of scent.

My passing sprang a bough, and bore
Its shelter guests away in a shower;
Autumn moths, harebell-azured, small
And lucid as a child's fingernail.

They hopped on the ground, fluttered, and
    rose
To cling on twigs or on my clothes:
So gentle and unwary of harm,
I cupped some in an anxious palm.

And then a gust of wind or whim
Breathed them over the chalkside rim
Till, watching from low lids a-stare,
I lost them in the vast of air.

While golden in the dusty green
The furze bells smouldered, I groped
    between
Dream and reality as I scanned
A smudge of blue dust on my hand.

C. DAY LEWIS

The Album

I see you, a child
In a garden sheltered for buds and playtime,
Listening as if beguiled
By a fancy beyond your years and the flowering maytime.
The print is faded: soon there will be
No trace of that pose enthralling,
Nor visible echo of my voice distantly calling
"Wait! Wait for me!"

Then I turn the page
To a girl who stands like a questioning iris
By the waterside, at an age
That asks every mirror to tell what the heart's desire is.
The answer she finds in that oracle stream
Only time could affirm or disprove,
Yet I wish I was there to venture a warning, "Love
Is not what you dream."

Next you appear
As if garlands of wild felicity crowned you—
Courted, caressed, you wear
Like immortelles the lovers and friends around you.
"They will not last you, rain or shine,
They are but straws and shadows,"
I cry: "Give not to those charming desperadoes
What was made to be mine."

One picture is missing—
The last. It would show me a tree stripped bare
By intemperate gales, her amazing
Noonday of blossom spoilt which promised so fair.
Yet, scanning those scenes at your heyday taken,
I tremble, as one who must view
In the crystal a doom he could never deflect—yes, I too
Am fruitlessly shaken.

I close the book;
But the past slides out of its leaves to haunt me
And it seems, wherever I look,
Phantoms of irreclaimable happiness taunt me.
Then I see her, petalled in new-blown hours,
Beside me—"All you love most there
Has blossomed again," she murmurs, "all that you missed
    there
Has grown to be yours."

Departure in the Dark

Nothing so sharply reminds a man he is mortal
As leaving a place
In a winter morning's dark, the air on his face
Unkind as the touch of sweating metal:
Simple goodbyes to children or friends become
A felon's numb
Farewell, and love that was a warm, a meeting place—
Love is the suicide's grave under the nettles.

Gloomed and clemmed as if by an imminent ice-age
Lies the dear world
Of your street-strolling, field-faring. The senses, curled
At the dead end of a shrinking passage,
Care not if close the inveterate hunters creep,
And memories sleep
Like mammoths in lost caves. Drear, extinct is the world,
And has no voice for consolation or presage.

There is always something at such times of the passover,
When the dazed heart
Beats for it knows not what, whether you part
From home or prison, acquaintance or lover—
Something wrong with the time-table, something unreal
In the scrambled meal
And the bag ready packed by the door, as though the heart
Has gone ahead, or is staying here for ever.

C. DAY LEWIS

No doubt for the Israelites that early morning
It was hard to be sure
If home were prison or prison home: the desire
Going forth meets the desire returning.
This land, that had cut their pride down to the bone
Was now their own
By ancient deeds of sorrow. Beyond there was nothing sure
But a desert of freedom to quench their fugitive yearnings.

At this blind hour the heart is informed of nature's
Ruling that man
Should be nowhere a more tenacious settler than
Among wry thorns and ruins, yet nurture
A seed of discontent in his ripest ease.
There's a kind of release
And a kind of torment in every goodbye for every man—
And will be, even to the last of his dark departures.

Sonnet

(from *O Dreams O Destinations*)

To travel like a bird, lightly to view
Deserts where stone gods founder in the sand,
Ocean embraced in a white sleep with land;
To escape time, always to start anew.
To settle like a bird, make one devoted
Gesture of permanence upon the spray
Of shaken stars and autumns; in a bay
Beyond the crestfallen surges to have floated.
Each is our wish. Alas, the bird flies blind,
Hooded by a dark sense of destination:
Her weight on the glass calm leaves no impression,
Her home is soon a basketful of wind.
Travellers, we're fabric of the road we go;
We settle, but like feathers on time's flow.

C. DAY LEWIS

Marriage of Two

So they were married, and lived
Happily for ever?
Such extravagant claims are not in heaven's gift—
Much less earth's, where love is chanceful as weather:
Say they were married, and lived.

Tell me his marriage vow.
Not the church responses,
But alone at a window one night saying, "Now
Let me be good to her, all my heart owns or wants is
Staked on this hazardous vow."

When was the marriage sealed?
One day the strange creature
He loved was missing; he found her, concealed
In a coign of, wearing the secret stamp of his nature.
So matings, if ever, are sealed.

How did the marriage end?
Some marriages die not.
The government goes into exile; then
The underground struggle is on, whose fighters fly not
Even at the bitter end.

What is the marriage of two?
The loss of one
By wounds or abdication; a true
Surrender mocked, an unwished victory won:
Rose, desert—mirage too.

Emily Brontë

All is the same still. Earth and heaven locked in
A wrestling dream the seasons cannot break:

C. DAY LEWIS

Shrill the wind tormenting my obdurate thorn trees,
Moss-rose and stonechat silent in its wake.
Time has not altered here the rhythms I was rocked in,
Creation's throb and ache.

All is yet the same, for mine was a country
Stoic, unregenerate, beyond the power
Of man to mollify or God to disburden—
An ingrown landscape none might long endure
But one who could meet with a passion wilder-wintry
The scalding breath of the moor.

All is yet the same as when I roved the heather
Chained to a demon through the shrieking night,
Took him by the throat while he flailed my sibylline
Assenting breast, and won him to delight.
O truth and pain immortally bound together!
O lamp the storm made bright!

Still on those heights prophetic winds are raving,
Heath and harebell intone a plainsong grief:
"Shrink, soul of man, shrink into your valleys—
Too sharp that agony, that spring too brief!
Love, though your love is but the forged engraving
Of hope on a stricken leaf!"

Is there one whom blizzards warm and rains enkindle
And the bitterest furnace could no more refine?
Anywhere one too proud for consolation,
Burning for pure freedom so that he will pine,
Yes, to the grave without her? Let him mingle
His barren dust with mine.

But is there one who faithfully has planted
His seed of light in the heart's deepest scar?
When the night is darkest, when the wind is keenest,
He, he shall find upclimbing from afar
Over his pain my chaste, my disenchanted
And death-rebuking star.

FRANCES BELLERBY

It is Not Likely Now

It is not likely now.
God's lion crouches low in jeopardy;
It is not likely that a step should sound
So late. Blame all on memory,
The tireless trickster who knows every path,
The way of every latch, mimics a pose in a chair
Truly to life, that the sad stranger Death
Stands back, awkward, and unfamiliar.

It is less likely now.
A great fleet jewels the sky tonight,
Ships silver-lamped, and green, yellow,
And ruby; and the whole vast sea of midnight
Theirs. Who that could ride with that fleet would return
Here? I would not. I would ride and ride forever,
My deep light brilliant on the dark ocean,
A sign for my harmless and forgotten lover.

It will soon be dawn now,
For the little wolf-wind whimpers like a child.
Why should I wait and wait who have never found,
Never, anything by waiting? And have won the right
To that flawless freedom which is death-in-life: freedom
Never to be welcomed nor to welcome; never to turn the head
And wave; nor for the mind to hare leaping home
In advance. The only treasure of the living dead.

Nothing is likely now.
An angel has flung back the futile stone
And lion-Christ, God's darling, strides freshly forth, done
Perhaps with death forever. Day without end?
But night is the flower of day; and at evening they come home
Who are coming. Count them on the thumb of one hand
Before you have finished, again evening will have come.

NORMAN CAMERON

The Thespians at Thermopylae

The honours that the people give always
Pass to those use-besotted gentlemen
Whose numskull courage is a kind of fear,
A fear of thought and of the oafish mothers
("Or with your shield or on it") in their rear.
Spartans cannot retreat. Why, then, their praise
For going forward should be less than ''others'''.
But we, actors and critics of one play,
Of sober-witted judgment, who could see
So many roads, and chose the Spartan way,
What has the popular report to say
Of us, the Thespians at Thermopylae?

The Disused Temple

When once the scourging prophet, with his cry
Of "money-changers" and "my Father's house",
Had set his mark upon it, men were shy
To enter, and the fane fell in disuse.

Since it was unfrequented and left out
Of living, what was there to do except
Make fast the door, destroy the key? (No doubt
One of our number did it while we slept.)

It stays as a disquieting encumbrance.
We moved the market-place out of its shade;
But still it overhangs our whole remembrance,
Making us both inquisitive and afraid.

Shrewd acousticians hammer on the door
And study from the echoes what is there;
Meaningless yet familiar, these appear
Much what we would expect—but we're not sure.

Disquiet makes us sleepy; shoddiness
Has come upon our crafts. No question that
We'll shortly have to yield to our distress,
Abandon the whole township, and migrate.

A Hook for Leviathan

"Ah, yes, the works are busy on the Hook
Designed to drag Leviathan from hiding.
'Not really mean it?' Why, man, have a look!
Ten thousand tons of steel along the siding,

"A billion cubic feet of foundry sand—
We've not collected all that stuff for play.
A project such as this, you'll understand,
Is not to be accomplished in a day.

"Think of the huge machine tools we'll employ
To cut the barbs: no metal's hard enough—
We're still kept waiting for the new alloy.
We'd have you know, Leviathan's jaws are tough.

"Then there's the little matter of the line—
Unprecedented problem of suspension.
A million strands, we've found, would be too fine.
We're making fresh experiments in tension."

And if one asks: "Where will you find the vessel
To carry such a hook?" the owners stare:
"Surely we have enough with which to wrestle.
We're not shipbuilders; that's not our affair."

REX WARNER

Sonnet

The understanding of a medical man
will forgive all, when all is understood,

and science and religion both are good
to explain away the villain, plot the plan
of what must be and is, and is therefore fine.
Yes, understanding is forgiveness. Yes,
I see it all, and there is no redress.
I recognise the stars that are not mine,
the important stars, the civilising light
by which to steer the boat and mark the day:
I see them beyond the fury of the sky,
shipwrecked and rolled from wave to wave of night,
sinking I see the certain fire and say:
"There are the useful stars, and here am I."

PETER QUENNELL

Procne

So she became a bird and bird-like danced
On a long sloe-bough, treading the silver blossom
With a bird's lovely feet,
And shaken blossoms fell into the hands
Of sunlight, and he held them for a moment
And let them drop.
And in the autumn Procne came again
And leapt upon the crooked sloe-bough singing
And the dark berries winked like earth-dimmed beads,
As the branch swung beneath her dancing feet.

While I Have Vision

While I have vision, while the glowing-bodied,
Drunken with light, untroubled clouds, with all this
    cold sphered sky,
Are flushed, above trees where the dew falls secretly,
Where no man goes, where beasts move silently,

PETER QUENNELL

As gently as light-feathered winds that fall
Chill among hollows filled with sighing grass,
While I have vision, while my mind is borne
A finger's length above reality,
Like that small plaining bird that drifts and drops
Among these soft-lapped hollows,
Robed gods, whose passing fills calm nights with
    sudden wind,
Whose spears still bar our twilight,
Bend and fill wind-shaken, troubled spaces with some
    peace,
With clear untroubled beauty,
That I may live, not chill and shrilling through
    perpetual day,
Remote, amazed, larklike, but may hold
The hours as firm, warm fruit,
This finger's length above reality.

JOHN BETJEMAN

The Old Liberals

Pale green of the *English Hymnal*! Yattendon hymns
    Played on the *hautbois* by a lady dress'd in blue
    Her white-haired father accompanying her thereto
On tenor or bass-recorder. Daylight swims
    On sectional book-case, delicate cup and plate
    And William de Morgan tiles around the grate
And many the silver birches the pearly light shines through.

I think such a running together of woodwind sound,
    Such painstaking piping high on a Berkshire hill,
    Is sad as an English autumn heavy and still,
Sad as a country silence, tractor-drowned;
For deep in the hearts of the man and the woman playing
    The rose of a world that was not has withered away.

Where are the wains with garlanded swathes a-swaying?
Where are the swains to wend through the lanes a-maying?
  Where are the blithe and jocund to ted the hay?
  Where are the free folk of England? Where are they?

Ask of the Abingdon bus with full load creeping
  Down into denser suburbs. The birch lets go
  But one brown leaf on browner bracken below.
Ask of the cinema manager. Night airs die
To still ripe scent of the fungus and wet woods weeping.
  Ask of the fish and chips in the Market Square.
  Here amid firs and a final sunset flare
Recorder and *hautbois* only moan at a mouldering sky.

Norfolk

How did the Devil come? When first attack?
  These Norfolk lanes recall lost innocence,
The years fall off and find me walking back
  Dragging a stick along the wooden fence
Down this same path where, forty years ago,
My father strolled behind me, calm and slow.

I used to fill my hand with sorrel seeds
  And shower him with them from the tops of stiles,
I used to butt my head into his tweeds
  To make him hurry down those languorous miles
Of ash and alder-shaded lanes, till here
Our moorings and the masthead would appear.

There after supper lit by lantern light
  Warm in the cabin I could lie secure
And hear against the polished sides at night
  The lap lap lapping of the weedy Bure,
A whispering and watery Norfolk sound
Telling of all the moonlit reeds around.

How did the Devil come? When first attack?
  The church is just the same, though now I know
Fowler of Louth restored it. Time, bring back
  The rapturous ignorance of long ago,
The peace before the dreadful daylight starts,
Of unkept promises and broken hearts.

Youth and Age on Beaulieu River, Hants

Early sun on Beaulieu water
    Lights the undersides of oaks,
Clumps of leaves it floods and blanches
All transparent glow the branches
    Which the double sunlight soaks;
    And to her craft on Beaulieu water
    Clemency the General's daughter
        Pulls across with even strokes.

Schoolboy-sure she is this morning;
    Soon her sharpie's rigg'd and free.
Cool beneath a garden awning
    Mrs. Fairclough, sipping tea
And raising large long-distance glasses
As the little sharpie passes,
    Sighs our sailor girl to see:

Tulip figure, so appealing,
    Oval face, so serious-eyed,
Tree-roots pass'd and muddy beaches,
On to huge and lake-like reaches,
    Soft and sun-warm, see her glide—
Slacks the slim young limbs revealing,
Sun-brown arm the tiller feeling—
    With the wind and with the tide.

Evening light will bring the water,
    Day-long sun will burst the bud,

Clemency the General's daughter,
Will return upon the flood.
But the older woman only
Knows the ebb-tide leaves her lonely
With the shining fields of mud.

A Subaltern's Love Song

Miss J. Hunter Dunn, Miss J. Hunter Dunn,
Furnish'd and burnish'd by Aldershot sun,
What strenuous singles we played after tea,
We in the tournament—you against me!

Love-thirty, love-forty, oh! weakness of joy,
The speed of a swallow, the grace of a boy,
With carefullest carelessness, gaily you won,
I am weak from your loveliness, Joan Hunter Dunn.

Miss Joan Hunter Dunn, Miss Joan Hunter Dunn,
How mad I am, sad I am, glad that you won.
The warm-handled racket is back in its press,
But my shock-headed victor, she loves me no less.

Her father's euonymus shines as we walk,
And swing past the summer-house, buried in talk,
And cool the verandah that welcomes us in
To the six-o'clock news and a lime-juice and gin.

The scent of the conifers, sound of the bath,
The view from my bedroom of moss-dappled path,
As I struggle with double-end evening tie,
For we dance at the Golf Club, my victor and I.

On the floor of her bedroom lie blazer and shorts
And the cream-coloured walls are be-trophied with
  sports,
And westering, questioning settles the sun
On your low-leaded window, Miss Joan Hunter Dunn.

JOHN BETJEMAN

The Hillman is waiting, the light's in the hall,
The pictures of Egypt are bright on the wall,
My sweet, I am standing beside the oak stair
And there on the landing's the light on your hair.

By roads "not adopted," by woodlanded ways,
She drove to the club in the late summer haze,
Into nine-o'clock Camberley, heavy with bells
And mushroomy, pine-woody, evergreen smells.

Miss Joan Hunter Dunn, Miss Joan Hunter Dunn,
I can hear from the car-park the dance has begun.
Oh! full Surrey twilight! importunate band!
Oh! strongly adorable tennis-girl's hand!

Around us are Rovers and Austins afar,
Above us, the intimate roof of the car,
And here on my right is the girl of my choice,
With the tilt of her nose and the chime of her voice.

And the scent of her wrap, and the words never said,
And the ominous, ominous dancing ahead.
We sat in the car park till twenty to one
And now I'm engaged to Miss Joan Hunter Dunn.

WILLIAM EMPSON

This Last Pain

This last pain for the damned the Fathers found:
"They knew the bliss with which they were not
    crowned."
  Such, but on earth, let me foretell,
  Is all, of heaven or of hell.

Man, as the prying housemaid of the soul,
May know her happiness by eye to hole:
  He's safe; the key is lost; he knows
  Door will not open, nor hole close.

WILLIAM EMPSON

"What is conceivable can happen too,"
Said Wittgenstein, who had not dreamt of you;
    But wisely; if we worked it long
    We should forget where it was wrong.

Those thorns are crowns which, woven into knots,
Crackle under and soon boil fool's pots;
    And no man's watching, wise and long,
    Would ever stare them into song.

Thorns burn to a consistent ash, like man;
A splendid cleanser for the frying-pan:
    And those who leap from pan to fire
    Should this brave opposite admire.

All those large dreams by which men long live well
Are magic-lanterned on the smoke of hell;
    This then is real, I have implied,
    A painted, small, transparent slide.

These the inventive can hand-paint at leisure,
Or most emporia would stock our measure;
    And feasting in their dappled shade
    We should forget how they were made.

Feign then what's by a decent tact believed
And act that state is only so conceived,
    And build an edifice of form
    For house where phantoms may keep warm.

Imagine, then, by miracle, with me,
(Ambiguous gifts, as what gods give must be)
    What could not possibly be there,
    And learn a style from a despair.

WILLIAM EMPSON

Letter I

You were amused to find you too could fear
"The eternal silence of the infinite spaces,"
That net-work without fish, that mere
Extended idleness, those pointless places
Who, being possiblized to bear faces,
Yours and the light from it, up-buoyed,
Even of the galaxies are void.

I approve, myself, dark spaces between stars;
All privacy's their gift; they carry glances
Through gulfs; and as for messages (thus Mars'
Renown for wisdom their wise tact enhances,
Hanged on the thread of radio advances)
For messages, they are a wise go-between,
And say what they think common-sense has seen.

Only, have we space, common-sense in common,
A tribe whose life-blood is our sacrament,
Physics or metaphysics for your showman,
For my physician in this banishment?
Too non-Euclidean predicament.
Where is that darkness that gives light its place?
Or where such darkness as would hide your face?

Our jovial sun, if he avoids exploding
(These times are critical), will cease to grin,
Will lose your circumambient foreboding;
Loose the full radiance his mass can win
While packed with mass holds all that radiance in;
Flame far too hot not to seem utter cold
And hide a tumult never to be told.

Villanelle

It is the pain, it is the pain, endures.
Your chemic beauty burned my muscles through.
Poise of my hands reminded me of yours.

What later purge from this deep toxin cures?
What kindness now could the old salve renew?
It is the pain, it is the pain, endures.

The infection slept (custom or change inures)
And when pain's secondary phase was due
Poise of my hands reminded me of yours.

How safe I felt, whom memory assures,
Rich that your grace safely by heart I knew.
It is the pain, it is the pain, endures.

My stare drank deep beauty that still allures.
My heart pumps yet the poison draught of you.
Poise of my hands reminded me of yours.

You are still kind whom the same shape immures.
Kind, and beyond adieu. We miss our cue.
It is the pain, it is the pain, endures.
Poise of my hands reminded me of yours.

Missing Dates

Slowly the poison the whole blood stream fills.
It is not the effort nor the failure tires.
The waste remains, the waste remains and kills.

It is not your system or clear sight that mills
Down small to the consequence a life requires;
Slowly the poison the whole blood stream fills.

They bled an old dog dry yet the exchange rills
Of young dog blood gave but a month's desires;
The waste remains, the waste remains and kills.

It is the Chinese tombs and the slag hills
Usurp the soil, and not the soil retires.
Slowly the poison the whole blood stream fills.

WILLIAM EMPSON

Not to have fire is to be a skin that shrills.
The complete fire is death. From partial fires
The waste remains, the waste remains and kills.

It is the poems you have lost, the ills
From missing dates, at which the heart expires.
Slowly the poison the whole blood stream fills.
The waste remains, the waste remains and kills.

VERNON WATKINS

First Joy

First joy through eye and limb
Shoots upward. Groundroots drive
Through shadow and crust a sheath.
I praise God with my breath
As hares leap, fishes swim,
And bees bring honey to the hive.

The yew shuts out that sky
And the dumbfounded well
Hides within its stone
The colours' trance; they shone
Pure, but the stones give cry
Answering what no colours spell.

First joy that sinks in the well
Falters to renew,
Slipping through listening hands
And lips of stone, where stands
Green Neptune, voice and veil
Uncoil from sleep the mysteries of
    the yew.

On the sands, children pick
Bright shells, who, stooping, know
Nothing of earth's white dead;
They run with graceful thread
Of light, and are made quick
By earlier streams that sweetlier flow.

Darkness divines great light.
Forced from what no child knows
Passionate joy springs up
Where death has choked the cup;
Even where blind fingers write,
Even where the gravestone's single
    flower blows.

Gravestones

Look down. The dead have life.
Their dreadful night accompanies our Springs.
Touch the next leaf:
Such darkness lives there, where a last grief sings.

Light blinds the whirling graves.
Lost under rainwet earth the letters run.
A finger grieves,
Touching worn names, bearing daughter and son.

Here the quick life was borne,
A fountain quenched, fountains with suffering crowned.
Creeds of the bone
Summoned from darkness what no Sibyl found.

Truly the meek are blest
Past proud men's trumpets, for they stilled their fame
Till this last blast
Gave them their muted, and their truest name.

Sunk are the stones, green-dewed,
Blunted with age, touched by cool, listening grass.
Vainly these died,
Did not miraculous silence come to pass.

Yet they have lovers' ends,
Lose to hold fast, as violets root in frost.
With stronger hands
I see them rise through all that they have lost.

I take a sunflower down,
With light's first faith persuaded and entwined.
Break, buried dawn,
For the dead live, and I am of their kind.

The Heron

The cloud-backed heron will not move:
He stares into the stream.
He stands unfaltering while the gulls
And oyster-catchers scream.
He does not hear, he cannot see
The great white horses of the sea,
But fixes eyes on stillness
Below their flying team.

How long will he remain, how long
Have the grey woods been green?
The sky and the reflected sky,
Their glass he has not seen,
But silent as a speck of sand
Interpreting the sea and land,
His fall pulls down the fabric
Of all that windy scene.

Sailing with clouds and woods behind,
Pausing in leisured flight,
He stepped, alighting on a stone,
Dropped from the stars of night.

He stood there unconcerned with day,
Deaf to the tumult of the bay,
Watching a stone in water,
A fish's hidden light.

Sharp rocks drive back the breaking waves,
Confusing sea with air.
Bundles of spray blown mountain-high
Have left the shingle bare.
A shipwrecked anchor wedged by rocks,
Loosed by the thundering equinox,
Divides the herded waters,
The stallion and his mare.

Yet no distraction breaks the watch
Of that time-killing bird.
He stands unmoving on the stone;
Since dawn he has not stirred.
Calamity about him cries,
But he has fixed his golden eyes
On water's crooked tablet,
On light's reflected word.

Peace in the Welsh Hills

Calm is the landscape when the storm has passed.
Brighter the fields, and fresh with fallen rain.
Where gales beat out new colour from the hills
Rivers fly faster, and upon their banks
Birds preen their wings, and irises revive.
Not so the cities burnt alive with fire
Of man's destruction: when their smoke is spent,
No phoenix rises from the ruined walls.

I ponder now the grief of many rooms.
Was it a dream, that age, when fingers found
A satisfaction sleeping in dumb stone,
When walls were built responding to the touch

In whose high gables, in the lengthening days,
Martins would nest? Though crops, though lives,
    would fail,
Though friends dispersed, unchanged the walls would
    stay,
And still those wings return to build in spring.

Here, where the earth is green, where heaven is true
Opening the windows, touched with earliest dawn,
In the first frost of cool September days,
Chrysanthemum weather, presaging great birth,
Who in his heart could murmur or complain:
"The light we look for is not in this land"?
That light is present and that distant time
Is always here, continually redeemed.

There is a city we must build with joy
Exactly where the fallen city sleeps.
There is one road through village, town and field,
On whose robust foundations Chaucer dreamed
A ride could wed the opposites in man.
There proud walls may endure, and low walls feed
The imagination if they have a vine
Or shadowy barn made rich with gathered corn.

Great mansions fear from their surrounding trees
The invasion of a wintry desolation
Filling their room with leaves. And cottages
Bring the sky down as flickering candles do,
Leaning on their own shadows. I have seen
Vases and polished brass reflect black windows
And draw the ceiling down to their vibrations.
Thick, deep and white-washed, like a bank of snow.

To live entwined in pastoral loveliness
May rest the eyes, throw pictures on the mind,
But most we need a metaphor of stone
Such as those painters had whose mountain-cities

VERNON WATKINS

Cast long low shadows on the Umbrian hills.
There, in some courtyard on the cobbled stone,
A fountain plays, and through a cherub's mouth
Ages are linked by water in the sunlight.

All of good faith that fountain may recall,
Woman, musician, boy, or else a scholar
Reading a Latin book. They seem distinct,
And yet are one, because tranquillity
Affirms the Judgement. So, in these Welsh hills,
I marvel, waking from a dream of stone,
That such a peace surrounds me, while the city
For which all long has never yet been built.

SHEILA WINGFIELD

Lines for the Margin of an Old Gospel

Children now awake to birds.
　Mortals rose to words
　　Fresh as the morning

When clover and the far hawks,
　Scabious and meadow-larks
　　Shadowed a searing

That ran along nerve and sense,
　To-mend a bad conscience
　　By caustic of loving.

Tax-collector and prostitute:
　Perhaps they were astute
　　More understanding

Than open throats, festered teeth,
　Slovenly wits and breath
　　Gaping and crowding,

Or than any tolling-tongued
   Masters who had wronged
      Life with their learning.

Gently or fiercely, to all around
   He would explain, expound,
      Like a dog leaping

Through tall stalks of wheat:
   Such was the pounce and feat
      Of this debating;

Till an attic room rang
   With a sad air sung
      After the supping.

Destiny and darkness flow
   Faster, now, than low
      Clouds that are falling;

His friend snores, head to rock;
   The world takes stock,
      Hardly breathing.

Thinking how steepled jealousy,
   Prim-lipped authority,
      Pride of condemning

Can derive from that despair,
   Sleep, lantern, unfair
      Act of denying,

Warmth drains out of us. The soul
   Shown in its goodness, whole:
      No hammering

Of flesh to wood can harm that proof.
   Yet man is without roof
      And night is freezing.

W. H. AUDEN

Lay Your Sleeping Head

Lay your sleeping head, my love,
Human on my faithless arm;
Time and fevers burn away
Individual beauty from
Thoughtful children, and the grave
Proves the child ephemeral:
But in my arms till break of day
Let the living creature lie,
Mortal, guilty, but to me
The entirely beautiful.

Soul and body have no bounds:
To lovers as they lie upon
Her tolerant enchanted slope
In their ordinary swoon,
Grave the vision Venus sends
Of supernatural sympathy,
Universal love and hope:
While an abstract insight wakes
Among the glaciers and the rocks
The hermit's sensual ecstasy.

Certainty, fidelity
On the stroke of midnight pass
Like vibrations of a bell,
And fashionable madmen raise
Their pedantic boring cry;
Every farthing of the cost,
All the dreaded cards foretell
Shall be paid, but from this night
Not a whisper, not a thought,
Not a kiss nor look be lost.

Beauty, midnight, vision dies:
Let the winds of dawn that blow
Softly round your dreaming head
Such a day of sweetness show
Eye and knocking heart may bless,
Find the mortal world enough;
Noons of dryness see you fed
By the involuntary powers,
Nights of insult let you pass
Watched by every human love.

Musée des Beaux Arts

About suffering they were never wrong,
The Old Masters: how well they understood
Its human position; how it takes place
While someone else is eating or opening a window or just
    walking dully along;
How, when the aged are reverently, passionately waiting
For the miraculous birth, there always must be
Children who did not specially want it to happen, skating
On a pond at the edge of the wood:
They never forgot
That even the dreadful martyrdom must run its course
Anyhow in a corner, some untidy spot
Where the dogs go on with their doggy life and the
    torturer's horse
Scratches its innocent behind on a tree.

In Brueghel's *Icarus*, for instance: how everything turns away
Quite leisurely from the disaster; the ploughman may
Have heard the splash, the forsaken cry,
But for him it was not an important failure; the sun shone
As it had to on the white legs disappearing into the green
Water; and the expensive delicate ship that must have seen
Something amazing, a boy falling out of the sky,
Had somewhere to get to and sailed calmly on.

W. H. AUDEN

Fish in the Unruffled Lakes

Fish in the unruffled lakes
The swarming colours wear,
Swans in the winter air
A white perfection have,
And the great lion walks
Through his innocent grove;
Lion, fish and swan
Act, and are gone
Upon Time's toppling wave.

We till shadowed days are done,
We must weep and sing
Duty's conscious wrong,
The Devil in the clock,
The Goodness carefully worn
For atonement or for luck;
We must lose our loves,
On each beast and bird that moves
Turn an envious look.

Sighs for folly said and done
Twist our narrow days;
But I must bless, I must praise
That you, my swan, who have
All gifts that to the swan
Impulsive Nature gave,
The majesty and pride,
Last night should add
Your voluntary love.

As I Walked Out One Evening

As I walked out one evening,
  Walking down Bristol Street,
The crowds upon the pavement
  Were fields of harvest wheat.

And down by the brimming river
  I heard a lover sing
Under an arch of the railway:
  "Love has no ending.

"I'll love you, dear, I'll love you
  Till China and Africa meet
And the river jumps over the mountain
  And the salmon sing in the street.

"I'll love you till the ocean
  Is folded and hung up to dry
And the seven stars go squawking
  Like geese about the sky.

"The years shall run like rabbits,
  For in my arms I hold
The Flower of the Ages
  And the first love of the world."

But all the clocks in the city
  Began to whirr and chime:
"O let not Time deceive you,
  You cannot conquer Time.

"In the burrows of the Nightmare
  Where Justice naked is,
Time watches from the shadow
  And coughs when you would kiss.

"In headaches and in worry
  Vaguely life leaks away,
And Time will have his fancy
  To-morrow or to-day.

"Into many a green valley
  Drifts the appalling snow;
Time breaks the threaded dances
  And the diver's brilliant bow.

'O plunge your hands in water,
Plunge them in up to the wrist;
Stare, stare in the basin
And wonder what you've missed.

"The glacier knocks in the cupboard
The desert sighs in the bed,
And the crack in the tea-cup opens
A lane to the land of the dead.

"Where the beggars raffle the banknotes
And the Giant is enchanting to Jack,
And the Lily-white Boy is a Roarer
And Jill goes down on her back.

"O look, look in the mirror,
O look in your distress;
Life remains a blessing
Although you cannot bless.

"O stand, stand at the window
As the tears scald and start;
You shall love your crooked neighbour
With your crooked heart."

It was late, late in the evening,
The lovers they were gone;
The clocks had ceased their chiming
And the deep river ran on.

from *In Memory of W. B. Yeats*

Earth, receive an honoured guest;
William Yeats is laid to rest:
Let the Irish vessel lie
Emptied of its poetry.

W. H. AUDEN

Time that is intolerant
Of the brave and innocent,
And indifferent in a week
To a beautiful physique,

Worships language and forgives
Everyone by whom it lives;
Pardons cowardice, conceit,
Lays its honours at their feet.

Time that with this strange excuse
Pardoned Kipling and his views,
And will pardon Paul Claudel,
Pardons him for writing well.

In the nightmare of the dark
All the dogs of Europe bark,
And the living nations wait,
Each sequestered in its hate;

Intellectual disgrace
Stares from every human face,
And the seas of pity lie
Locked and frozen in each eye.

Follow, poet, follow right
To the bottom of the night,
With your unconstraining voice
Still persuade us to rejoice;

With the farming of a verse
Make a vineyard of the curse,
Sing of human unsuccess
In a rapture of distress;

In the deserts of the heart
Let the healing fountain start,
In the prison of his days
Teach the free man how to praise

W. H. AUDEN

The Unknown Citizen

To

JS/07/M/378

THIS MARBLE MONUMENT IS ERECTED BY
THE STATE

He was found by the Bureau of Statistics to be
One against whom there was no official complaint,
And all the reports on his conduct agree
That, in the modern sense of an old-fashioned word, he was a
    saint,
For in everything he did he served the Greater Community.
Except for the War till the day he retired
He worked in a factory and never got fired,
But satisfied his employers, Fudge Motors Inc.
Yet he wasn't a scab or odd in his views,
For his Union reports that he paid his dues,
(Our report on his Union shows it was sound)
And our Social Psychology workers found
That he was popular with his mates and liked a drink.
The Press are convinced that he bought a paper every day
And that his reactions to advertisements were normal in every
    way.
Policies taken out in his name prove that he was fully insured,
And his Health-card shows he was once in hospital but left it
    cured.
Both Producers Research and High-Grade Living declare
He was fully sensible to the advantages of the Instalment Plan
And had everything necessary to the Modern Man,
A gramophone, a radio, a car and a frigidaire.
Our researchers into Public Opinion are content
That he held the proper opinions for the time of year;
When there was peace, he was for peace; when there was war, he
    went.
He was married and added five children to the population,

Which our Eugenist says was the right number for a parent of
   his generation,
And our teachers report that he never interfered with their
   education.
Was he free? Was he happy? The question is absurd:
Had anything been wrong, we should certainly have heard.

JOHN LEHMANN

The Sphere of Glass

So through the sun-laced woods they went
Where no one walked but two that day,
And they were poets, and content
Sharing the one deep-vistaed way,
Sister and brother, to walk on
Where years like thickets round them lay.

It was the Roman dyke that ran
Between the bluebells and the fern,
The loam so fresh, they half began
To feel the bones deep under turn,
And, listening, dreamed their argument
Something from ancient death would learn.

One bird among the golden-green
Spangle of leaves was poised to sing:
They heard the opening trill, and then
Silence, as if its heart could bring
No note so pure but would disturb
The soundless fountain of the Spring.

Within the wood, within that hour
It seemed a sphere of glass had grown
That glittered round their lives with power
To link what grief the dyke had known
With voices of their vaster war
The sunshot bombers' homing drone,

And make one tragic harmony
Where still this theme, their hope, returned,
And still the Spring unchangeably
In fires of its own sap was burned,
And poetry, from love and death,
The peace their human contest earned.

It might have been all history
Without the sphere of wonder lay
And just beyond their colloquy
Some truth more pure than they could say,
While through the bluebells and the fern
Sister and brother made their way.

The Last Ascent

We cried: Good luck! and watched them go
Over the hayfields in the sun;
Then dreaming of their happiness,
We waited till the day was done,

And we could greet them, tired and gay,
Returning to the supper laid
Where on the wildflowers round the porch
The apple branches shook their shade.

Night came: but there was still no sign.
We sent the children to their bed,
And lit the lamp, and spoke no more,
Still waiting, with bewildered dread.

An hour before the moon should rise,
We heard their feet drag through the grass:
Their clothes were torn, their cheeks had bled,
And as we ran to aid, "Alas,

"The ice-bound steep," they sighed, "betrayed:
That last ascent! The inhuman skies!"
We looked at one another then
With question frozen in our eyes—

"We did not guess, no angel warned
How cruel the eagles and ravines!"
Where had they wandered? What mirage
Had lured beyond our farmland scenes?

There was no mountain there, no snow,
No glacier where the eagle hovers,
No deep ravine or dizzy fall
To scar and shock: but they were lovers.

A Death in Hospital

On the first day, the lifted siege at last
On starving hope: his spirit dropped its load,
And turning once more to the world of friends
   Wept for the love they showed.

Then on the second day, like a black storm
Terror of death burst over him, and pain
Pierced like the jagged lightning, in whose flash
   All he would never gain—

The wine-blue inlets of a home restored,
Peace, and the growth of love in summer's field,
And loaded baskets from a poet's tree—
   Pitiless, stood revealed.

The third night there was battle in the skies:
The tongues of all the guns were hot with steel,
The groaning darkness shuddered, but could add
   No wrench to his ordeal.

JOHN LEHMANN

The fourth day, when they came with daffodils
And sea-borne fruit, and honey from his home,
They seemed but shadows, where he choked and fought
   There was so little room.

It was the fifth day explanation broke:
There was no fear, nor human longing more,
And all his life in that surprising dawn
   Appeared a dwindling shore

Separate for ever from his tide-kissed boat,
An isle with all its gardens fondly kept
Complete and curious, that belonged to them,
   His friends, who stayed and wept.

LOUIS MACNEICE

June Thunder

The Junes were free and full, driving through tiny
Roads, the mudguards brushing the cow-parsley,
Through fields of mustard and under boldly embattled
     Mays and chestnuts

Or between beeches verdurous and voluptuous
Or where broom and gorse beflagged the chalkland—
All the flare and gusto of the unenduring
     Joys of a season

Now returned but I note as more appropriate
To the maturer mood impending thunder
With an indigo sky and the garden hushed except for
     The treetops moving.

Then the curtains in my room blow suddenly inward,
The shrubbery rustles, birds fly heavily homeward,
The white flowers fade to nothing on the trees and rain
  comes
     Down like a dropscene.

175

Now there comes the catharsis, the cleansing downpour
Breaking the blossoms of our overdated fancies,
Our old sentimentality and whimsicality,
　　　Loves of the morning.

Blackness at half-past eight, the night's precursor,
Clouds like falling masonry and lightning's lavish
Annunciation, the sword of the mad archangel
　　　Flashed from the scabbard.

If only you would come and dare the crystal
Rampart of rain and the bottomless moat of thunder,
If only now you would come I should be happy
　　　Now if now only.

Meeting Point

　　Time was away and somewhere else,
　　There were two glasses and two chairs
　　And two people with the one pulse
　　(Somebody stopped the moving stairs):
　　Time was away and somewhere else.

　　And they were neither up nor down,
　　The stream's music did not stop
　　Flowing through heather, limpid brown,
　　Although they sat in a coffee shop
　　And they were neither up nor down.

　　The bell was silent in the air
　　Holding its inverted poise—
　　Between the clang and clang, a flower,
　　A brazen calyx of no noise:
　　The bell was silent in the air.

The camels crossed the miles of sand
That stretched around the cups and plates;
The desert was their own, they planned
To portion out the stars and dates:
The camels crossed the miles of sand.

Time was away and somewhere else.
The waiter did not come, the clock
Forgot them and the radio waltz
Came out like water from a rock:
Time was away and somewhere else.

Her fingers flicked away the ash
That bloomed again in tropic trees:
Not caring if the markets crash
When they had forests such as these,
Her fingers flicked away the ash.

God or whatever means the Good
Be praised that time can stop like this,
That what the heart has understood
Can verify in the body's peace
God or whatever means the Good.

Time was away and she was here
And life no longer what it was,
The bell was silent in the air
And all the room a glow because
Time was away and she was here.

The Springboard

He never made the dive—not while I watched.
High above London, naked in the night
Perched on a board. I peered up through the bars
Made by his fear and mine but it was more than fright
That kept him crucified among the budding stars.

Yes, it was unbelief. He knew only too well
That circumstances called for sacrifice
But, shivering there, spreadeagled above the town,
His blood began to haggle over the price
History would pay if he were to throw himself down.

If it would mend the world, that would be worth while
But he, quite rightly, long had ceased to believe
In any Utopia or in Peace-upon-Earth;
His friends would find in his death neither ransom nor
    reprieve
But only a grain of faith—for what it was worth.

And yet we know he knows what he must do.
There above London where the gargoyles grin
He will dive like a bomber past the broken steeple,
One man wiping out his own original sin
And, like ten million others, dying for the people.

Explorations

The whale butting through scarps of moving marble,
The tapeworm probing the intestinal darkness,
The swallows drawn collectively to their magnet,
    These are our prototypes and yet,
Though we may envy them still, they are merely patterns
    To wonder at—and forget.

For the ocean-carver, cumbrous but unencumbered,
Who tired of land looked for his freedom and frolic in water,
Though he succeeded, has failed; it is only instinct
    That plots his graph and he,
Though appearing to us a free and happy monster, is merely
    An appanage of the sea.

And the colourless blind worm, triumphantly self degraded,
Who serves as an image to men of the worst adjustment—

LOUIS MACNEICE

Oxymoron of parasitical glory—
    Cannot even be cursed,
Lacking the only pride of his way of life, not knowing
    That he has chosen the worst.

So even that legion of birds who appear so gladly
Purposeful, with air in their bones, enfranchised
Citizens of the sky and never at odds with
    The season or out of line,
Can be no model to us; their imputed purpose
    Is a foregone design—

And ours is not. For we are unique, a conscious
Hoping and therefore despairing creature, the final
Anomaly of the world, we can learn no method
    From whales or birds or worms;
Our end is our own to be won by our own endeavour
    And held on our own terms.

from *The Kingdom*

A little dapper man but with shiny elbows
And short keen sight, he lived by measuring things
And died like a recurring decimal
Run off the page, refusing to be curtailed;
Died as they say in harness, still believing
In science, reason, progress. Left his work
Unfinished *ipso facto* which continued
Will supersede his name in the next text-book
And relegate him to the anonymous crowd
Of small discoverers in lab or cloister
Who link us with the Ice Age. Obstinately
He canalised his fervour, it was slow
The task he set himself but plotting points
On graph paper he felt the emerging curve
Like the first flutterings of an embryo

In somebody's first pregnancy; resembled
A pregnant woman too in that his logic
Yet made that hidden child the centre of the world
And almost a messiah; so that here
Even here over the shining test-tubes
The spirit of the alchemist still hovered
Hungry for magic, for the philosopher's stone.
And Progress—is that magic too? He never
Would have conceded it, not even in these last
Years of endemic doubt; in his perspective
Our present tyrants shrank into parochial
Lords of Misrule, cross eddies in a river
That has to reach the sea. But has it? Who
Told him the sea was there?
Maybe he told himself and the mere name
Of Progress was a shell to hold to the ear
And hear the breakers burgeon. Rules were rules
And all induction checked but in the end
His reasoning hinged on faith and the first axiom
Was oracle or instinct. He was simple
This man who flogged his brain, he was a child;
And so, whatever progress means in general,
He in his work meant progress. Patiently
As Stone Age man he flaked himself away
By blocked-out patterns on a core of flint
So that the core which was himself diminished
Until his friends complained that he had lost
Something in charm or interest. But conversely
His mind developed like an ancient church
By the accretion of side-aisles and the enlarging of
  lights
Till all the walls are windows and the sky
Comes in, if coloured; such a mind . . . a man . . .
Deserves a consecration; such a church
Bears in its lines the trademark of the Kingdom.

E. J. SCOVELL

An Elegy

In early winter before the first snow
When the earth shows in garden beds
(For the foam is blown of flower-heads
And the gardener has cut low
Or tied in place the stock and green)
When the world wears an inward mien
Of mourning and of deprivation,
The appearance fits this time and nation.

In early winter before the first snow,
The child whose steps began in June
In the short misty afternoon
Walks in the mournful park below
Branches of trees, and standing stretches
Her arms and sings her wordless catches.
Like light her play and happiness
Flicker on the world's distress.

In this city still unraided
Where the queues stretch round the corners
It befits us to be mourners
Who read of other lands invaded,
Who have heard at night death pass
To northern cities over us.
It befits us who live on
To consider and to mourn.

The quiet days before the snow,
The child's feet on the yellowing grass—
How can I make a rite of these
To mourn the pang I do not know,
Death fastened on the life of man?
Sorrow uses what it can.
Take as my rite this winter tune:
The child's walk in the darkening afternoon.

E. J. SCOVELL

Bloody Cranesbill on the Dunes

We saw one first and thought it was the only one
For beauty made this flower seem to be alone
As stars burn each alone in gulfs of time and space.
And opening distance like a star, with sunset face
Broken through earth as angels part the clouds, it made appear
The grass a firmament, confusing far and near.

As the evening star was not and is suddenly
On the fresh lawn of heaven, the clear, unbroken sea—
Not made with hands, not born, it shines, not says "I am"—
So the one flower seemed in the grass, the shell-heart flame.

But the night ripens and another star
Takes body where none seemed in the ghost-laden air;
And summoned to men's sight, exorcized to lay down
Invisibility, they crowd our vision,
Thicker than birds or bees, than clover leaves or stones;
And hands of children gather these solitary ones.

For most alone is most accompanied.
I watched the ballet dancer's lonely, floating steps and head
Proud, meek as one unborn, and wondering saw that she
Was compassed with her solitary kind, a galaxy.

So walking through the dunes the second day, we found
Another cranesbill flower, a world sprung from the ground;
And there a third and fourth, and further on the source,
The blood-tipped seeds, the opened rosy flowers,
There risen in time, a freshet flooding; strange and hard to see
As if they had been always known, yet could not be.

An Open Air Performance of "As You Like It"

Art is unmade
To nature and the wild again
On the scythed grass before

E. J. SCOVELL

A lime and skeletal ash
And the wall, solid with flowering,
Of longer unmown grass
Fumy with parsley flowers,
A level mist rising;
Where the young actors barefoot,
Warm in their exaltation
Burn in the evening's chill.

The art the poet won
From wilderness dissolves again,
Unformed upon this formless stage
Confluent with all earth's air;
For infiltrating winds,
Laughter, mid-distant trains
Steal the speech from their voices,
Being amateur, unsure,
And moths bemuse their faces,
And our attention loses
Stragglers to cloud and star.

Envoys of life
At their set hour the swifts fly over
Possess the air above us
And fish-tailed, fast as sight,
Play in their foamy margins,
Their intertidal light;
While the flood lamps yet hardly
Sophisticate earth's colours,
And we half ride with the birds
Over our audience faces,
Over the reckless words.

And when "If you have been . . ."
Orlando cries, "If ever been
Where bells have knolled to church . . ."
And sweet upon his words

E. J. SCOVELL

The Christ Church evening bell
Answers the homesick youth
Like rhyme confirming verse,
Evidence crowning truth,
It seems to our delight
As though the poet's earth
And ours lay in one night;

As though we had heard
The bell before the words were made
With him. Therefore I love
All loose ends, distractions
At such performances,
All their imperfections;
And if we bring our children,
Their soft and stubborn questions
Threading the marble words;
And art delivered up
To nature and the wild again.

JULIAN BELL

Pluviose

At the black wood's corner, not one green bud
On the oak, but the boughs weeping
In steady rain, bright drops.
Low clouds, through all
The wet day fall.
Gurgling ditch, by the copse;
Down the rushy furrow seeping,
Comes the water, running through hoof-poached mud.
Stream and pond cream-brown with the loam:
The outlet swirling with heaped foam.
Noisily through
Hatches and culverts, leaping, goes
The stream that to the water meadows
Runs, and floods blue.

JULIAN BELL

Woods and Kestrel

The quiet woods in the hot Eastertide
Sleep to the dancing chime of village bells,
Under the scarp of the tall down that swells
To a steep shouldered crest on the north side.

The gas thin film of green leaves, wreathing smoke
In the black trees, sap swelling in the heat:
Wet empty axe-cropped clearing at their feet,
Where moss-banked primroses in the sun soak.

Deep from the hill the opened floor appears,
White scattered chips and face ridgèd boles
Of the felled trees; stacked ash and hazel poles,
Where they have cut the copse, as each ten years.

A kestrel, umber mantle and black wings,
From the bare down, out of the empty skies,
Deep into the wooded hollow, kite-winged, flies,
And in curved line, down through the tree-tops, swings.

Thence comes the steel flash of an axe's head,
Stooping in hawk-swift curve of metal bright
On soft wood, the sap-moist chips spurting white.
Up the slow hill the ringing bell thuds spread.

With sunshine in brown eyes, on rippling breast,
The kestrel up and away from the axe stroke lifts,
And swirling up the blue weald landscape shifts
To the forest ridge's pine-wood darkened crest.

JOCELYN BROOKE

Three Barrows Down

In those fields haunted by fear
And a memory of soldiers—
Where the white road curves
From the blackened mill
By Ileden and Womenswold
Towards the tree-capped hill—

There in those summer-gold
And wide-flung pastures
The ear is cozened still
By the bare and empty song
Of evil forgotten days
And echo of ancient wrong;

And walking in the old ways
By the high banks and hedges
I come again to the dark
Three-barrowed wood and hear
In the summer-haunted stillness
That litany of fear;

And like a subtle illness
Invading blood and tissue,
From fields far and near
Creeps the rank smell of fighting,
The infection of the squaddies'
Bare-limbed and red-faced hating:

Whose muscled, belted bodies
Straddle the ditch and hedgeside
With rawboned violence, waiting
For the dark, predestined hour—
The harsh and bitter seeding
Of the dragon-rooted flower.

JOCELYN BROOKE

Their eyes unheeding
Of storm-dark horizon,
And white-capped water-tower
Pricking the sullen line
Of the wood whose trees conceal
Tombs of an older time.

O betony and self-heal
Be near to salve the wounds
Of warrior and rookie
In the embattled hour:
And give to the queer and lonely
The brief and phallic power

To conquer and be only
Unkind to the swing-fed bloke
And pious white-faced sergeant
Who in the vernal hour
With evil would revoke
The dawn, the springing flower.

KATHLEEN RAINE

Nocturne

Night comes, an angel stands
measuring out the time of stars,
still are the winds, and still the hours.

It would be peace to lie
still in the still hours at the angel's feet,
upon a star hung in a starry sky,
but hearts another measure beat.

Each body, wingless as it lies,
sends out its butterfly of night
with delicate wings and jewelled eyes.

And some upon day's shores are cast,
and some in darkness lost
in waves beyond the world, where float
somewhere the islands of the blest.

Seen in a Glass

Behind the tree, behind the house, behind the stars
Is the presence that I cannot see
Otherwise than as house and stars and tree.

Tree, house and stars
Extend to infinity within themselves
Into the mystery of the world

Where whirl the wheels of power whose pulses beat
Out of nothing, out of night,
Leaves, stones and fires,

The living tree whose maypole dance
Of chromosome and nucleus
Traces the maze of boughs and leaves,

The standing house of stone that poured
In molten torrent when was hurled
Out of chaos this great world,

And suns whose kindling begins anew
Or ends the course that tree, house, world move through,

Upheld by being that I cannot know
In other form than stars and stones and trees
Assume in nature's glass, in nature's eyes.

KATHLEEN RAINE

Seventh Day

Passive I lie, looking up through leaves,
An eye only, one of the eyes of earth
That open at a myriad points at a living surface.
Eyes that earth opens see and delight
Because of the leaves, because of the unfolding of the leaves.
The folding, veining, imbrication, fluttering, resting,
The green and deepening manifold of the leaves.

Eyes of the earth know only delight
Untroubled by anything that I am, and I am nothing:
All that nature is, receive and recognize,
Pleased with the sky, the falling water and the flowers,
With bird and fish and the striations of stone.
Every natural form, living and moving
Delights these eyes that are no longer mine
That open upon earth and sky pure vision.
Nature sees, sees itself, is both seer and seen.

This is the divine repose, that watches
The ever-changing light and shadow, rock and sky and ocean.

JAMES REEVES

Old Crabbed Men

This old crabbed man, with his wrinkled, fusty clothes
And his offensive smell—who would suppose
That in his day he invented a new rose,
Delightful still to a fastidious eye and nose?

That old crabbed man, pattering and absurd,
With a falsetto voice—which of you has heard
How in his youth he mastered the lyric word
And wrote songs faultless as those of a spring bird?

JAMES REEVES

This old crabbed man, sloven of speech and dress,
Was once known among women—who would now guess?—
As a lover of the most perfect address,
Reducing the stubbornest beauty to nakedness.

That old crabbed man, a Herod of the first water,
His manhood consumed in bragging, drink, and slaughter,
The terror of fag, bearer, batman, caddy, porter,
Is the adored of his one infant great-granddaughter.

From such crabbed men—should we not realise?—
Despite their present insupportable guise,
May have been distilled something apt, sweet or wise,
Something pleasing perhaps to former minds or eyes.

W. R. RODGERS

Carol

Deep in the fading leaves of night
There lay the flower that darkness knows,
Till winter stripped and brought to light
The most incomparable Rose
That blows, that blows.

The flashing mirrors of the snow
Keep turning and returning still:
To see the lovely child below
And hold him is their only will;
Keep still, keep still.

And to let go his very cry
The clinging echoes are so slow
That still his wail they multiply
Though he lie singing now below,
So low, so low.

Even the doves forget to grieve
And gravely to his greeting fly
And the lone places that they leave
All follow and are standing by
On high, on high.

White Christmas

Punctually at Christmas the soft plush
Of sentiment snows down, embosoms all
The sharp and pointed shapes of venom, shawls
The hills and hides the shocking holes of this
Uneven world of want and wealth, cushions
With cosy wish like cot on-wool the cool
Arm's-length interstices of caste and class,
And into obese folds subtracts from sight
All truculent acts, bleeding the world white.

Punctually that glib pair, Peace and Goodwill,
Emerge royally to take the air,
Collect the bows, assimilate the smiles,
Of waiting men. It is a genial time.
Angels, like stalactites, descend from heaven,
Bishops distribute their own weight in words,
Congratulate the poor on Christlike lack,
And the member for the constituency
Feeds the five thousand, and has plenty back.

Punctually to-night, in old stone circles
Of set reunion, families stiffly sit
And listen; this is the night, and this the happy time
When the tinned milk of human kindness is
Upheld and holed by radio-appeal.
Hushed are hurrying heels on hard roads,
And every parlour's a pink pond of light
To the cold and travelling man going by
In the dark, without a bark or a bite.

But punctually to-morrow you will see
All this silent and dissembling world
Of silted sentiment suddenly melt
Into mush and watery welter of words
Beneath the warm and moving traffic of
Feet and actual fact. Over the stark plain
The stilted mill-chimneys once again spread
Their sackcloth and ashes, a flowing mane
Of repentance for the false day that's fled.

BERNARD SPENCER

Yachts on the Nile

Like air on skin, coolness of yachts at mooring,
a white flung handful;
fresh as a girl at her rendezvous, and wearing
frou-frou names, Suzy, Yvette or Gaby,
lipped by the current, uttering
the gay conversation of their keels.

Lovely will be their hesitant leaving of
the shore for the full stream,
fingering the breeze down out of the sky; then leaning
as a player leans his cheek to the violin
—that strange repose of power—
and the race will hold them like a legend.

Terrible their perfection: and theirs I saw
like clouds covering the Solent
when I was a boy: and all those sails that dip
ages back in the hardly waking mind;
white visitors of islands,
runners on the turf of rivers.

What these ask with their conquering look and speed
written in their bodies like birds,
is our ecstasy, our tasting as if a dish
magnificence of hazard, cunning of the tiller-hand,
a freedom: and it is by something
contrary in being human

That I look for a distant river, a distant woman,
and how she carried her head:
the great release of the race interns me here . . .
and it may be, too, we are born with some nostalgia
to make the migration of sails
and wings a crying matter.

Greek Excavations

Over the long-shut house
Which earth, not keys kept under watch,
I prod with a stick and down comes rattling soil
Into the dug out room;
And pottery comes down,
Hard edges of drinking vessels, jars for oil,
Mere kitchen stuff, rubbish of red and brown,
Stubble of conquests.

—And I suddenly discover this discovered town.
The wish of the many, their abused trust,
Blows down here in a little dust,
So much unpainted clay;
The minimum wish
For the permanence of the basic things of a life,
For children and friends and having enough to eat
And the great key of a skill;
The life the generals and the bankers cheat.

Peering for coin or confident bust
Or vase in bloom with the swiftness of horses,

BERNARD SPENCER

My mind was never turned the way
Of the classic of the just and the unjust.
I was looking for things which have a date,
And less of the earth's weight,
When I broke this crust.

STEPHEN SPENDER

Polar Exploration

Our single purpose was to walk through snow
With faces swung to their prodigious North,
Like compass needles. As clerks in whited banks
Leave bird-claw pen-prints columned on white paper,
On snow we added footprints.
Extensive whiteness drowned
All sense of space. We tramped through
Static, glaring days, Time's suspended blank.
That was in Spring and Autumn. Summer struck
Water over rocks, and half the world
Became a ship with a deep keel, the booming floes
And icebergs with their little birds:
Twittering Snow Bunting, Greenland Wheatear,
Red-throated Divers; imagine butterflies,
Sulphurous cloudy yellow; burnish of bees
That suck from saxifrage; crowberry,
Bilberry, cranberry, *Pyrola Uniflora*.
There followed winter in a frozen hut
Warm enough at the kernel, but dare to sleep
With head against the wall—ice gummed my hair!
Hate Culver's loud breathing, despise Freeman's
Fidget for washing: love only the dogs
That whine for scraps, and scratch. Notice
How they run better (on short journeys) with a bitch.
In that, different from us.

Return, return, you warn! We do. There is
Your city, with railways, money, words, words, words.
Meals, papers, exchanges, debates,
Cinema, wireless: then there is Marriage.
I cannot sleep. At night I watch
A clear voice speak with words like drawing.
Its questions are white rifts:—Was
Ice, our rage transformed? The raw, the motionless
Skies, were these the Spirit's hunger?
The continual hypnotized march through snow,
The dropping nights of precious extinction, were these
Only the wide circuits of the will,
The frozen heart's evasions? If such thoughts seem
A kind of madness here, a coldness
Of snow like sheets in summer—is the North
Over there, a palpable, true madness,
A solid simplicity, absolute, without towns,
Only with bears and fish, a raging eye,
A new and singular sex?

The Room Above the Square

The light in the window seemed perpetual
When you stayed in the high room for me;
It glowed above the trees through leaves
Like my certainty.

The light is fallen and you are hidden
In sunbright peninsulas of the sword:
Torn like leaves through Europe is the peace
That through us flowed.

Now I climb alone to the high room
Above the darkened square
Where among stones and roots, the other
Unshattered lovers are.

STEPHEN SPENDER

Two Armies

Deep in the winter plain, two armies
Dig their machinery, to destroy each other.
Men freeze and hunger. No one is given leave
On either side, except the dead, and wounded.
These have their leave; while new battalions wait
On time at last to bring them violent peace.

All have become so nervous and so cold
That each man hates the cause and distant words
That brought him here, more terribly than bullets.
Once a boy hummed a popular marching song,
Once a novice hand flapped their salute;
The voice was choked, the lifted hand fell,
Shot through the wrist by those of his own side.

From their numb harvest, all would flee, except
For discipline drilled once in an iron school
Which holds them at the point of the revolver.
Yet when they sleep, the images of home
Ride wishing horses of escape
Which herd the plain in a mass unspoken poem.

Finally, they cease to hate: for although hate
Bursts from the air and whips the earth with hail
Or shoots it up in fountains to marvel at,
And although hundreds fall, who can connect
The inexhaustible anger of the guns
With the dumb patience of those tormented animals?

Clean silence drops at night, when a little walk
Divides the sleeping armies, each
Huddled in linen woven by remote hands.
When the machines are stilled, a common suffering
Whitens the air with breath and makes both one
As though these enemies slept in each other's arms.

Only the lucid friend to aerial raiders
The brilliant pilot moon, stares down
Upon this plain she makes a shining bone
Cut by the shadows of many thousand bones.
Where amber clouds scatter on No-Man's-Land
She regards death and time throw up
The furious words and minerals which destroy.

Seascape

(*In Memoriam M.A.S.*)

There are some days the happy ocean lies
Like an unfingered harp, below the land.
Afternoon gilds all the silent wires
Into a burning music for the eyes.
On mirrors flashing between fine-strung fires
The shore, heaped up with roses, horses, spires,
Wanders on water, walking above ribbed sand.

The motionlessness of the hot sky tires
And a sigh, like a woman's, from inland
Brushes the instrument with shadowing hand
Drawing across its wires some gull's sharp cries
Or bell, or shout, from distant, hedged-in shires;
These, deep as anchors, the hushing wave buries.

Then from the shore, two zig-zag butterflies,
Like errant dog-roses, cross the bright strand
Spiralling over sea in foolish gyres
Until they fall into reflected skies.
They drown. Fishermen understand
Such wings sunk in such ritual sacrifice,

Recalling legends of undersea, drowned cities.
What voyagers, oh what heroes, flamed like pyres
With helmets plumed, have set forth from some island

And them the sea engulfed. Their eyes,
Contorted by the cruel waves' desires
Glitter with coins through the tide scarcely scanned,
While, above them, that harp assumes their sighs.

The Trance

Sometimes, apart in sleep, by chance,
You fall out of my arms, alone,
Into the chaos of your separate trance.
My eyes gaze through your forehead, through the bone,
And see where in your sleep distress has torn
Its violent path, which on your lips is shown
And on your hands and in your dream forlorn.

Restless, you turn to me, and press
Those timid words against my ear
Which thunder at my heart like stones.
"Mercy," you plead. Then "Who can bless?"
You ask. "I am pursued by Time," you moan.
I watch that precipice of fear
You tread, naked in naked distress.

To that deep care we are committed
Beneath the wildness of our flesh
And shuddering horror of our dream,
Where unmasked agony is permitted.
Our bodies, stripped of clothes that seem,
And our souls, stripped of beauty's mesh,
Meet their true selves, their charms outwitted.

This pure trance is the oracle
That speaks no language but the heart,
Our angel with our devil meets
In the atrocious dark nor do they part
But each each forgives and greets,
And their mutual terrors heal
Within our married miracle.

198

LYNETTE ROBERTS

These Words I Write on Crinkled Tin

To the green wood where I found my love:
To the green wood where I held my love:
To the green wood now my love is gone.

I follow death that stands on my breath,
My heart cut out by the timeless scythe,
All grievous foliage stifling and still.
I carve marks on the bark's rough edge
To convince my grief he came here once
Whose spirit shivers the aspen tree.

To the green wood where the woodcock flies,
To the green wood where the nightjar hides,
To the green wood with red eyes of a dove.

The young jays springing and curious
Who peck eyes from the lamb's sweet face,
Resemble too well my heartless step.
For he loves me and I love another,
I love another yet he still loves me,
He loves me still yet I love another.

To the green wood where the green air fades;
To the green wood fluid with icy shades;
To the green wood afraid I follow fast:

Past Syrian Juniper and tall grass;
Hanging with dark secrets the Brewer's spruce;
The pond that drew the young child in;
Among darkening leaves: a nightingale
Sobbing in the sunniest season,
"My love, My love, do I love the other?"

To the green wood where I found my love;
To the green wood where I held my love;
To the green wood now my love is gone.

HAL SUMMERS

A Valentine

At one point of the journey, a memorable one,
The train ran out of the tunnel under the down
And look, it was a new country, we had outrun
All vestige at last of the pursuing town.

The train ran quietly under a sky of jade;
There could not be a metropolis under that sky;
Each side was a hanging field of such deep shade
It was the mind greened it and not the eye.

At the moment a thing seems memorable, and yet
Though the memory be retentive and true the heart,
We begin almost immediately to forget;
The sand-castle is washed away, part by part.

Then there is another moment: I open the door,
Enter the lighted house, out of the weather,
And look, a new country—this I journeyed for:
I come to you, speak to you, we are together.

This moment also and so all moments fade,
Like a piano's chord, loud, evanescent.
Waves of brightness rill into cold shade.
We can be safe neither in past nor present.

Love calls continually for life's whole power;
Either it must be renewed or it must die.
Each hour we are new souls: o love, each hour
Meet me the first time, say me last good-bye.

On the Cliff

Cloud-riders leap for Normandy,
The opulent sun in his grandstand
Looks on, the dark and shaggy sea
Worries the white bone of the land.

HAL SUMMERS

Who made me an arbiter? May I
Not follow as wind and season lead?
There is no verdict in the sky
Nor in the growing of the seed.

The mind of nature changes ever,
Ever renews: o let me yield
My rigid thought, flow as a river
Or rivery shadows on the weald;

Live like the blossom on these branches
Flaming and falling as times pass
Or like the obedient moon that blanches
The unrebellious fields of grass;

With children's welcome see the day
Closing the volume of the dark
And listen in the innocent way
To the high quavers of the lark;

Passive let me, when blind night fingers
Its braille of stars, that light receive
While in my ear unchallenged lingers
The owl's lugubrious semibreve.

Clouds at the water-jump fly fraught
With hazardous light: come good or ill,
Ring off now, rest, protesting thought,
And let the judging mind be still.

RAYNER HEPPENSTALL

St. Stephen's Word

The little Jack of Christ
Come to its arrogant crown
In solitude and unrest
Will bear the spirit down.

RAYNER HEPPENSTALL

Stones break upon the skin,
The soul's integument,
And I could laugh to scorn
A death of Heaven's intent.

Before that face's rock,
The struts of that nostrilled head,
It was joy that my heart should break
And I in the law lie dead.

But I saw Heaven's decree
Moisten the tight lips of Saul
And the joy of the law turn away
On the broken legs of St. Paul.

In a world of little men
My sweetness drips from that spire
Of dry stone to impregnate
Regions of no desire.

PAUL DEHN

Fern House at Kew

Look! it is as though the sun,
Defrosting every spangled pane,
Should touch the ïern engraven there
And turn it green again;
    Till the fronds, uncurling in
      The ice which held them captive, flow
      With water-music from the roof
    To tropic airs below;
And I, the boy who many a night
Fashioned in a jungle dream
The boat that I may never steer
Darkly against the stream,
    Quant the fathomed gangways, now,
    Brushed by all green things that grow.

PAUL DEHN

Pondweed, here, without a pond
Wavers on the stagnant air,
Soft beside the trailing hand
Drifts the maidenhair
    And steeply to the lightless stream
    The tributary moonwort flows,
    Distilling on the river-bed
    A green light that glows.
Yet, by the cataract, how still
The prehistoric tendrils rise:
Antennae of enormous moth,
Spider with spores for eyes.
    Diluvian images, they stand
    Unstirring in an older land.

O yellow-hammered sun, my bird
In Paradise beyond the cage,
Sing to the fossil mind, unscale
The lizard eye of age;
    Till fireflies, juggling in the dark
    Above the duckboard ripples, turn
    Candescent as the speckled light
    That filters through the fern;
And humming birds in splendour thread
The tapestry a dreamer wove,
Slinging their scarlet shuttles through
The green warp of the grove.
    Now, behind the tall bamboo,
    Tiger lurks, and cockatoo.

The clock strikes one. A shadow falls
On serpent-stripe and tortoiseshell.
The toucan lifts his melon beak
In token of farewell;
    For waterfowl are calling on
    The English ornamental pool,
    Where carrot-coloured goldfish swim
    And prams are put to cool.

PAUL DEHN

Close the door. Nor ever look
Behind you in the fronded pane.
Orpheus lost Eurydice,
And I must find again
   The little star-crossed boy at play
   A continent of years away.

ROY FULLER

The Giraffes

I think before they saw me the giraffes
Were watching me. Over the golden grass,
The bush and ragged open tree of thorn,
From a grotesque height, under their lightish horns,
Their eyes were fixed on mine as I approached them.
The hills behind descended steeply: iron
Coloured outcroppings of rock half covered by
Dull green and sepia vegetation, dry
And sunlit: and above, the piercing blue
Where clouds like islands lay or like swans flew.

Seen from those hills the scrubby plain is like
A large-scale map whose features have a look
Half menacing, half familiar, and across
Its brightness arms of shadow ceaselessly
Revolve. Like small forked twigs or insects move
Giraffes, upon the great map where they live.

When I went nearer, their long bovine tails
Flicked loosely, and deliberately they turned,
An undulation of dappled grey and brown,
And stood in profile with those curious planes
Of neck and sloping haunches. Just as when
Quite motionless they watched I never thought
Them moved by fear, a desire to be a tree,

So as they put more ground between us I
Saw evidence that these were animals with
Perhaps no wish for intercourse, or no
Capacity.
          Above the falling sun
Like visible winds the clouds are streaked and spun,
And cold and dark now bring the image of
Those creatures walking without pain or love.

The Petty Officers' Mess

Just now I visited the monkeys: they
Are captive near the mess. And so the day
Ends simply with a sudden darkness, while
Again across the palm trees, like a file,
    The rain swings from the bay.

The radio speaks, the lights attract the flies,
Above them and the rain our voices rise,
And somewhere from this hot and trivial place
As the news tells of death, with pleasant face,
    Comes that which is not lies.

The voices argue: *Soldiers in the end*
Turn scarecrows; their ambiguous figures blend
With all who are obsessed by food and peace.
The rulers go, they cannot order these
    Who are not disciplined.

O cars with abdicating princes: streets
Of untidy crowds: O terrible defeats!
Such images which haunt us of the past
Flash on the present like the exile's vast
    Shivers and fleshy heats;

But never coincide. Do they approach?
Upon that doubt I'm frightened to encroach—
Show me, I say, *the organizations that*
Will change the rags and mob into the state,
  Like pumpkin into coach.

The voices make no answer. Music now
Throbs through the room and I remember how
The little pickaxe shapes of swallows swerve
From balconies and whitewashed walls; a curve
  Of bird-blue bay; a dhow:

Small stabbing observations! And I know
(The cheap song says it on the radio)
That nerves and skin first suffer when we part,
The deep insensitive tissues of the heart
  Later, when time is slow.

And time has done his part and stands and looks
With dumb exasperated face. The books
Year after year record the crisis and
The passion, but no change. The measuring sand
  Is still. There are no flukes,

Like the virtuous sulphonamides, to kill
The poisons of the age, but only will:
Reduction of desires to that cold plan
Of raping the ideal; the new frail man
  Who slays what's in the hill.

The monkeys near the mess (where we all eat
And dream) I saw tonight select with neat
And brittle fingers dirty scraps, and fight,
And then look pensive in the fading light,
  And after pick their feet.

They are secured by straps about their slender
Waists, and the straps to chains. Most sad and tender
They clasp each other and look round with eyes
Like ours at what their strange captivities
  Invisibly engender.

ROY FULLER

The Image

A spider in the bath. The image noted:
Significant maybe but surely cryptic.
A creature motionless and rather bloated,
The barriers shining, vertical and white:
Passing concern, and pity mixed with spite.

Next day with some surprise one finds it there.
It seems to have moved an inch or two, perhaps.
It starts to take on that familiar air
Of prisoners for whom time is erratic.
The filthy aunt forgotten in the attic.

Quite obviously it came up through the waste,
Rejects through ignorance or apathy
That passage back. The problem must be faced;
And life go on though strange intruders stir
Among its ordinary furniture.

One jibs at murder, so a sheet of paper
Is slipped beneath the accommodating legs.
The bathroom window shows for the escaper
The lighted lanterns of laburnum hung
In copper beeches—on which scene it's flung.

We certainly would like thus easily
To cast out of the house all suffering things.
But sadness and responsibility
For our own kind lives in the image noted:
A half-loved creature, motionless and bloated.

Translation

Now that the barbarians have got as far as Picra,
And all the new music is written in the twelve tone scale,
And I am anyway approaching my fortieth birthday,
   I will dissemble no longer.

ROY FULLER

I will stop expressing my belief in the rosy
Future of man, and accept the evidence
Of a couple of wretched wars and innumerable
    Abortive revolutions.

I will cease to blame the stupidity of the slaves
Upon their masters and nurture, and will say,
Plainly, that they are enemies to culture,
    Advancement and cleanliness.

From progressive organisations, from quarterlies
Devoted to daring verse, from membership of
Committees, from letters of various protest
    I shall withdraw forthwith.

When they call me reactionary I shall smile
Secure in another dimension. When they say
"Cinna has ceased to matter" I shall know
    How well I reflect the times.

The ruling class will think I am on their side
.And make friendly overtures, but I shall retire
To the side furthest from Picra and write some poems
    About the doom of the whole boiling.

Anyone happy in this age and place
Is daft or corrupt. Better to abdicate
From a material and spiritual terrain
    Fit only for barbarians.

F. T. PRINCE

The Babiaantje

Hither, where tangled thickets of the acacia
Wreathed with a golden powder, sigh
And when the boughs grow dark, the hoopoe
Doubles his bell-like cry,

Spreading his bright-striped wings and brown crest
Under a softening spring sky,—
I have returned because I cannot rest,
And would not die.

Here it was as a boy that, I remember,
I wandered ceaselessly, and knew
Sweetness of spring was in the bird's cry,
And in the hidden dew
The unbelievably keen perfume
Of the Babiaantje, a pale blue
Wild hyacinth that between narrow grey leaves
On the ground grew.

The flower will be breathing there now, should I wish
To search the grass beneath those trees,
And having found it, should go down
To snuff it, on my knees.
But now, although the crested hoopoe
Calls like a bell, how barren these
Rough ways and dusty woodlands look to one
Who has lost youth's peace!

The Question

And so we two came where the rest have come,
To where each dreamed, each drew, the other home
From all distractions to the other's breast,
Where each had found, each was, the wild bird's nest.
For that we came, and knew that we must know
The thing we knew of but we did not know.

We said then, What if this were now no more
Than a faint shade of what we dreamed before?
If love should here find little joy or none,
And done, it were as if it were not done,
Would we not love still? What if none can know
The thing we know of but we do not know?

For we know nothing but that, long ago,
We learnt to love God whom we cannot know.
I touch your eyelids that one day must close,
Your lips as perishable as a rose:
And say that all must fade, before we know
The thing we know of but we do not know.

Soldiers Bathing

The sea at evening moves across the sand.
Under a reddening sky I watch the freedom of a band
Of soldiers who belong to me. Stripped bare
For bathing in the sea, they shout and run in the warm air;
Their flesh, worn by the trade of war, revives
And my mind towards the meaning of it strives.

All's pathos now. The body that was gross,
Rank, ravenous, disgusting in the act or in repose,
All fever, filth and sweat, its bestial strength
And bestial decay, by pain and labour grows at length
Fragile and luminous. "Poor bare forked animal,"
Conscious of his desires and needs and flesh that rise and fall,
Stands in the soft air, tasting after toil
The sweetness of his nakedness: letting the sea-waves coil
Their frothy tongues about his feet, forgets
His hatred of the war, its terrible pressure that begets
A machinery of death and slavery,
Each being a slave and making slaves of others: finds that he
Remembers lovely freedom in a game,
Mocking himself, and comically mimics fear and shame.

He plays with death and animality.
And reading in the shadows of his pallid flesh, I see
The idea of Michelangelo's cartoon
Of soldiers bathing, breaking off before they were half done
At some sortie of the enemy, an episode
Of the Pisan wars with Florence. I remember how he showed

Their muscular limbs that clamber from the water,
And heads that turn across the shoulder, eager for the slaughter,
Forgetful of their bodies that are bare,
And hot to buckle on and use the weapons that are lying there.
—And I think too of the theme another found
When, shadowing men's bodies on a sinister red ground,
Another Florentine, Pollaiuolo,
Painted a naked battle: warriors straddled, hacked the foe,
Dug their bare toes into the ground and slew
The brother-naked man who lay between their feet and drew
His lips back from his teeth in a grimace.

They were Italians who knew war's sorrow and disgrace
And showed the thing suspended, stripped: a theme
Born out of the experience of war's horrible extreme
Beneath a sky where even the air flows
With *lacrimae Christi*. For that rage, that bitterness, those blows,
That hatred of the slain, what could it be
But indirectly or directly a commentary
On the Crucifixion? And the picture burns
With indignation and pity and despair by turns,
Because it is the obverse of the scene
Where Christ hangs murdered, stripped upon the Cross. I mean,
That is the explanation of its rage.

And we too have our bitterness and pity that engage
Blood, spirit in this war. But night begins
Night of the mind: who nowadays is conscious of our sins?
Though every human deed concerns our blood,
And even we must know, what nobody has understood,
That some great love is over all we do,
And that is what has driven us to this fury, for so few
Can suffer all the terror of that love:
The terror of that love has set us spinning in this groove
Greased with our blood.
                              These dry themselves and dress,
Combing their hair, forget the fear and shame of nakedness.
Because to love is frightening we prefer

The freedom of our crimes. Yet, as I drink the dusky air,
I feel a strange delight that fills me full,
Strange gratitude, as if evil itself were beautiful,
And kiss the wound in thought, while in the west
I watch a streak of red that might have issued from Christ's
    breast.

ANNE RIDLER

The Speech of the Dead

News of the dead is heard through words of the living.
After a casual phrase
Sometimes we burn with tears to recognize
Familiar words of the dead,
And Never again Never again cries against the loving
    greeting;
News of the dead, but by the living heard as
Dead news, and no true meeting.

No twittering ghosts, they speak as they always did,
But through our lips. Do they pursue and haunt us,
Or is it we who haunt them with the past, and will not rid
Their glory of that obsessive ghost?
O, in the sharp pale beams of the winter air
We seem to breathe their element, and the cold stir
About the brain is their interior speech.
They haunt us, and we them,
But it is our sad yearning that keeps them out of reach.

Those words out of the past that gave us pain
For the present, those are still our spirits' exchange,
But sounding through them now, most deeply-felt,
A death- and a life-time's loss and gain.

The blind to each of their four senses add
A little skill and so atone for the fifth.
Might we, for that blind lack in not being dead,
Atone by greater silence and the skill
To guess and be still.
Not to imagine them sharing this or that
Our temporal activity, and turn
Their supernatural state to ours, but
To know them as they are through what we know they were;
And in that glory of love to learn
Words of the dead through living lips a prayer.

The Phoenix Answered

Sitting in this garden you cannot escape symbols,
    Take them how you will.
      Here on the lawn like an island where the wind is still,
        Circled by tides in the field and swirling trees,
        It is of love I muse,
Who designs the coloured fronds and heavy umbels,
          Second-hand marriage, not for passion but business,
          Brought on by the obliging bees.

This hedge is a cool perch for the brown turtle-dove,
    His phoenix unseen:
    Such was their love that perhaps they grew to be one
      At first the mystical making love in marriage
      Had all my heart and my homage:
A fire and a fusion were what I wanted of love.
        But bodies are separate, and her fanatic bliss
        Left the phoenix bodiless.

Frosty burning cloud, delectable gate
    Of heaven hopelessly far,
    Though tilting almost to touch, whose holy fire
      Has no corrosive property unless
      Despair of it destroys us;

ANNE RIDLER

When we love, towards you our faces are set.
　　Once I would win by the pains of passion alone,
　　Aim at you still, that method outgrown.

If daily love now takes from these earlier ones
　　The sweetness without the pain,
　　The burning nights, the breathless fears gone,
　　　Peace in their place I never hoped to be given
　　　Unless if ever in heaven—
This is your own success, who have at once
　　　The unscathing fire and the ease of peace,
　　　All that I praise and bless.

R. S. THOMAS

Enigma

A man is in the fields, let us look with his eyes,
As the first clouds ripen with the sunrise,
At the earth around us, marking the nameless flowers
That minister to him through the tedious hours
Of sweat and toil, their grave, half-human faces
Lifted in vain to greet him where he passes.
The wind ruffles the meadow, the tall clouds sail
Westward full-rigged, and darken with their shadow
The bright surface as a thought the mind.
The earth is beautiful, and he is blind
To it all, or notices only the weeds' way
Of wrestling with and choking the young hay
That pushes tentatively from the gaunt womb.
He cannot read the flower-printed book
Of nature, nor distinguish the small songs
The birds bring him, calling with wide bills,
Out of the leaves and over the bare hills;
The squealing curlew and the loud thrush
Are both identical, just birds, birds;
He blames them sullenly as the agreed,
Ancestral enemies of the live seed,

Unwilling to be paid by the rich crop
Of music swelling thickly to the hedge top.

Blind? Yes, and deaf, and dumb, and the last irks most,
For could he speak, would not the glib tongue boast
A lore denied our neoteric sense,
Being handed down from the age of innocence?
Or would the cracked lips, parted at last, disclose
The embryonic thought that never grows?

Farm Child

Look at this village boy, his head is stuffed
With all the nests he knows, his pockets with flowers,
Snail-shells and bits of glass, the fruit of hours
Spent in the fields by thorn and thistle tuft.
Look at his eyes, see the harebell hiding there;
Mark how the sun has freckled his smooth face
Like a finch's egg under that bush of hair
That dares the wind, and in the mixen now
Notice his poise; from such unconscious grace
Earth breeds and beckons to the stubborn plough.

GEORGE BARKER

Summer Song 1

I looked into my heart to write
    And found a desert there.
But when I looked again I heard
Howling and proud in every word
    The hyena despair.

Great summer sun, great summer sun,
    All loss burns in trophies;

And in the cold sheet of the sky
Lifelong the fishlipped lovers lie
  Kissing catastrophes.

O loving garden where I lay
  When under the breasted tree
My son stood up behind my eyes
And groaned: Remember that the price
  Is vinegar for me.

Great summer sun, great summer sun,
  Turn back to the designer:
I would not be the one to start
The breaking day and the breaking heart
  For all the grief in China.

My one, my one, my only love,
  Hide, hide your face in a leaf,
And let the hot tear falling burn
The stupid heart that will not learn
  The everywhere of grief.

Great summer sun, great summer sun,
  Turn back to the never-never
Cloud-cuckoo, happy, far-off land
Where all the love is true love, and
  True love goes on for ever.

Verses for the 60th Birthday of T. S. Eliot

I

By that evening window where
His accurate eye keeps Woburn Square
Under perpetual judgement so
That only the happy can come and go
About these gardens and not be
Tested in that dark neutrality.
Which, in between love and disgust,
Hates most of all its own mistrust,

GEORGE BARKER

I see this gentle and gothic man
Tame Apollyon with a pen.

2

I never know the juggernauts
Go bulldozing through my thoughts
So that everything I own
Is trod down and overthrown
Without remembering that worse
Than thunder in the hearse
Is the supernatural sigh
Of illusions as they die—
But in the room of Eliot
The visions whistle as they rot.

3

To him the dead twig in the gutter
Cries across all law to utter
Confidences that would bring
Tears to the eyes of anything.
But that set imperial face
Has looked down on our disgrace
And, without betraying so
Little as a twinge of sorrow,
Seen all grief begin again—
A gentle and long-suffering man.

4

Outside the huge negations pass
Like whirlwinds writing on the grass
Inscriptions teaching us that all
The lessons are ephemeral;
But as the huge negations ride
And depredate all things outside
His window, he puts out his hand
And writes with whirlwinds on the ground
Asseverations that tame
The great negations with his name.

GEORGE BARKER

Letter to a Young Poet

There is that whispering gallery where
A dark population of the air
Gives back to us those vocables
We dare not robe in syllables:

I speak of the whispering gallery
Of all Dionysian poetry
Within whose precincts I have heard
An apotheosis of the word

As down those echoing corridors
The Logos rode on a white horse;
Till every No that sense could express
Turned to a transcendental Yes.

Sanctified by such passages
Let us exchange our messages,
And, as we walk, all enigmas
Describe themselves in terms of stars.

From those lyrical waterfalls rise
Words that bring rainbows to the eyes
And memories called up from the ground
Smile to see their blood around.

There is a spirit of turbulence
Inhabiting the intelligence
Determined always to impose
Another reason on the rose

Another cause upon the creature
Than the privilege of its nature;
A handcuff and a history
Upon all natural mystery

And this turbulent spirit starts
That insurrection in our hearts
By which the laws of poetry
Are broken into anarchy:

The anarchy that seeks to show
An altitude which way to go,
Or use astronomy to prove
That duty is our only love.

But over the known world of things
The great poem folds its wings
And from a bloody breast will give
Even to those who disbelieve.

By the known world the intellect
Stands with its bright gun erect,
But the long loving verities
Are kissing at the lattices.

That dark population of the air
Leans downward, singing, to declare
The mystery of the world is this:
That we do not know what is.

Channel Crossing

And just by crossing the short sea
To find the answer sitting there
Combing out its snaky hair
And with a smile regarding me
Because it knows only too well
That I shall never recognize
The axioms that I should prize
Or the lies that I should tell.

I saw the question in the sky
Ride like a gull to fool me, as
The squat boat butted at the seas
As grossly as through ultimates I
Churn up a frothy wake of verbs
Or stir up a muddy residue
Looking for that answer who
Sanctifies where she perturbs.

The horror of the questionmark
I looked back and saw stand over
The white and open page of Dover
Huge as the horn of a scapegoat. Dark
It stood up in the English day
Interrogating Destiny
With the old lip of the sea:
"What can a dead nation say?"

As these words wailed in the air
I looked at Europe and I saw
The glittering instruments of war
Grow paler but not go from where
Like a Caesarian sunset on
The cold slab of the horizon
They lay foretelling for tomorrow
Another day of human sorrow.

But when I turned and looked into
The silent chambers of the sea
I saw the displaced fishes flee
From nowhere into nowhere through
Their continent of liberty.
O skipping porpoise of the tide
No longer shall the sailors ride
You cheering out to sea.

I thought of Britain in its cloud
Chained to the economic rocks
Dying behind me. I saw the flocks
Of great and grieving omens crowd

About the lion on the stone.
And I heard Milton's eagle mewing
Her desolation in the ruin
Of a great nation, alone.

That granite and gigantic sigh
Of the proud man beaten by
Those victories from which we die;
The gentle and defeated grief
Of the gale that groans among
Trees that are a day too strong
And, victorious by a leaf,
Show the winner he was wrong.

The continent of discontent
Rose up before me as I stood
Above the happy fish. Endued
With hotter and unhappier blood
Contented in my discontent,
I saw that every man's a soul
Caught in the glass wishing bowl:
To live at peace in discontent.

O somewhere in the seven leagues
That separate us from the stricken
Amphitheatre of the spirit,
O somewhere in that baleful sea
The answer of sad Europe lodges,
The clue that causes us to sicken
Because we cannot find and share it,
Or, finding, cannot see.

So in the sky the monstrous sun
Mocked like a punishment to be,
Extending now, to you and me
The vision of what we have done:
And as the boat drew to the quay
I thought, by crossing the short water
I shall not find, in its place,
The answer with a silent face.

PATRIC DICKINSON

The Hounds

The hounds. The great man's dream. The stone.
Let me alone, there's the fire to light,
The garden to dig, the shoes to clean.
The hounds. The great man's dream. The stone.
And nobody knows what the words mean,
But they know me. They are poems to write.

I wrote the mnemonics down and thought,
But I will cheat them, they can wait,
I will choose my time and place to meet them.
I wrote the mnemonics down and thought,
I have locked them in, I can forget them.
But the key sang to the lock, "Too late".

One died in prison, one escaped,
But the third is out and dangerous,
(Don't you believe his half of the story)
One died in prison, one escaped,
But the third is changed to a ruthless fury
And says it was I that wrought the change.

What I saw was the Harriers
At exercise on an August morning
Like an Alken print, quite innocent.
What I saw was the Harriers
And to write without any hidden warning
In what I saw was all I meant.

The hounds. The great man's dream. The stone.
But Orestes knows what I must write,
He knows I see them and what they mean:
The hounds. The great man's dream. The stone.
Has nobody any shoes to clean?
Has nobody got a fire to light?

PATRIC DICKINSON

The Swallows

For two I know

Have the swallows come?
The swallows have come to tell us
How often we have said inside ourselves
"I shall not go this year . . . I shall wait . . ."

But the heart has flown, has left
The body like a book or a map
Marked *England, instinct, Africa, migrancy,*
That tells us nothing but a dead-reckoning.

Swallows flying blind,
Against whose flight the head winds howl
   "too late!",
Where shall you, what shall you find?
No instrument of the mind
Can bring you safely to the landing place.

Yet it is there, beaconing, beckoning,
Onward inward until
You break the navel-seal of Single Shape
And are the Continent of Being
You came from and return to,
Beyond the maps of Will.

O loving fingerprint unique
On a heart flown from how far
To build its clay house under these eaves
This one domestic breast
Instinct of soul believes
Is the right resting place!

PATRIC DICKINSON

—And then to feel beloved lips upon the face
Imprint a kiss so old that bodies shake
The chain of living back to its last link—
(*O terror of the slave who knows*
His Africa of longing lost
If the chain break!)

Dear flyers from the climate of your dream
Here is the place to wake.

LAWRENCE DURRELL

To Ping-Kû, Asleep

You sleeping child asleep, away
Between the confusing world of forms,
The lamplight and the day; you lie
And the pause flows through you like glass
Asleep in the body of the nautilus.

Between comparison and sleep,
Lips that move in quotation;
The turning of a small blind mind
Like a plant everywhere ascending.
Now our love has become a beanstalk.

Invent a language where the terms
Are smiles; someone in the house now
Only understands warmth and cherish,
Still twig-bound, learning to fly.

This hand exploring the world makes
The diver's deep-sea fingers on the sills
Of underwater windows; all the wrecks
Of our world where the sad blood leads back
Through memory and sense like divers working.

LAWRENCE DURRELL

Sleep my dear, we won't disturb
You, lying in the zones of sleep.
The four walls symbolize love put about
To hold in silence which so soon brims
Over into sadness; it's still dark.

Sleep and rise a lady with a flower
Between your teeth and a cypress
Between your thighs: surely you won't ever
Be puzzled by a poem or disturbed by a poem
Made like fire by the rubbing of two sticks?

Nemea

A song in the valley of Nemea:
Sing quiet, quite quiet here.

Song for the brides of Argos
Combing the swarms of golden hair:
Quite quiet, quiet there.

Under the rolling comb of grass,
The sword outrusts the golden helm.

Agamemnon under tumulus serene
Outsmiles the jury of skeletons:
Cool under cumulus the lion queen:

Only the drums can celebrate,
Only the adjective outlive them.

A song in the valley of Nemea:
Sing quiet, quiet, quiet here.

Tone of the frog in the empty well,
Drone of the bald bee on the cold skull,

Quiet, Quiet, Quiet.

LAWRENCE DURRELL

In the Garden: Villa Cleobolus

The mixtures of this garden
Conduct at night the pine and oleander,
Perhaps married to dust's thin edge
Or lime where the cork tree rubs
The quiet house, bruising the wall:

And dense the block of thrush's notes
Press like a bulb and keeping time
In this exposure to the leaves,
And as we wait the servant comes,

A candle shielded in the warm
Coarse coral of her hand, she weaves
A pathway for her in the golden leaves,
Gathers the books and ashtrays in her arm
Walking towards the lighted house,

Brings with her from the uninhabited
Frontiers of the darkness to the known
Table and tree and chair
Some half-remembered passage from a fugue
Played from some neighbour's garden
On an old horn-gramophone,

And you think: if given once
Authority over the word,
Then how to capture, praise or measure
The full round of this simple garden
All its nonchalance at being,
How to adopt and raise its pleasure?

Press as on a palate this observed
And simple shape, like wine?
And from the many undeserved
Tastes of the mouth select the crude
Flavour of fruit in pottery
Coloured among this lovely neighbourhood?

LAWRENCE DURRELL

Beyond, I mean, this treasure hunt
Of selves, the pains we sort to be
Confined within the loving chamber of a form,
Within a poem locked and launched
Along the hairline of the normal mind?

Perhaps not this: but somehow, yes,
To outflank the personal neurasthenia
That lies beyond in each expiring kiss:
Bring joy, as lustrous on this dish
The painted dancers motionless in play
Spin for eternity, describing for us all
The natural history of the human wish.

CLIFFORD DYMENT

The Temple

Luke tells us how the boy Jesus
Was missed on his return to Galilee:
He had tarried in the Temple, zealous to learn
What His Father's will was to be.

I think of this page in Luke now.
I have left the soldiery to march ahead
And I lie here, the hawthorn budding,
The celandines like stars about my head.

This morning I surprised a stoat
Feasting on the blood of a hare
And now, all around me, epithalamions of birds
Vibrate in the air.

I ponder: some million years ago
Forests and crying fearful beasts perished
When a sea shuddered and threw up a mountain
To make a hill on which I rest.

227

Must death create? I speak
My question in this Temple under the sky—
But no answer comes from stoat or bird or hill
Whether it is man's Cross to kill, or die.

The Children

Quietly the children wait
With eyes that shine like knives
Brightening the fading world
Through which I daily walk
My grown uncertain way from death to life.

Untaught and unafraid
They watch with their blades bare,
Blades where appetite glistens
As on visionary tongues
Keen to cut at a world that tastes so new.

Once, a child, I waited
Like children waiting now;
I, too, had surgeon's eyes
That instantaneously
Severed from time all time except tomorrow.

I, too, looked at the parents
Making a home for me;
Using trowel and timber
But more their heart and brain:
I saw a home that I was bound to destroy.

I am the builder now
As once my father built,
Using his trowel and timber
And some of his heart and brain
To build a home unlike his but the same—

And quietly the children wait,
Their eyes shining like knives
Brightening the fading world
Through which I daily walk
My grown uncertain way from life to death.

NORMAN NICHOLSON

Wales

Walking on the step of the shingle, here
Where the curlew follows the scallop of bay
And halts and prods the sand,
Looking beyond the cormorant's thoroughfare,
Beyond the drift and dip of the sea,
I saw the hills of Wales like stone clouds stand.

The sea flowed round them and the sky
Flowed under, and the floating peaks
Were frozen high in air;
I was a child then, and the winters blew
Mist across the skyline and spray against the rocks,
But blew open that window into Wales no more.

This year as a neighbour I looked at Wales;
Saw the sun on the rocks and the wind in the bracken,
And the telegraph poles like a boundary fence
Straddle the combe between the hills,
And westward from England and the Wrekin
Saw shadows of clouds advance.

But the sun was hot on the limbs, the turf on the heels,
The berries were fat as grapes, and the way
Bent back on the Shropshire side of the border—
I walked no nearer Wales,
But returned to wait by the former sea,
Aware that the mist will never lift to order.

NORMAN NICHOLSON

To a Child Before Birth

This summer is your perfect summer. Never will the skies
So stretched and strident be with blue
As these you do not see; never will the birds surprise
With such light flukes the ferns and fences
As these you do not hear. This year the may
Smells like rum-butter, and day by day
The petals slip from the cups like lover's hands,
Tender and tired and satisfied. This year the haws
Will form as your fingers form, and when in August
The sun first stings your eyes,
The fruit will be red as brick and free to the throstles.
Oh but next year the may
Will have its old smell of plague about it; next year
The songs of the birds be selfish, the skies have rain;
Next year the apples will be tart again.
But do not always grieve
For the unseen summer. Perfection is not the land you leave,
It is the pole you measure from; it gives
Geography to your ways and wanderings.
What is your perfection is another's pain;
And because she in impossible season loves
So in her blood for you the bright bird sings.

The Undiscovered Planet

Out on the furthest tether let it run
Its hundred-year-long orbit, cold
As solid mercury, old and dead
Before this world's fermenting bread
Had got a crust to cover it; landscape of lead
Whose purple voes and valleys are
Lit faintly by a sun
No nearer than a measurable star.

No man has seen it; the lensèd eye
That pin-points week by week the same patch of sky
Records not even a blur across its pupil; only
The errantry of Saturn, the wry
Retarding of Uranus, speak
Of the pull beyond the pattern:
The unknown is shown
Only by a bend in the known.

Millom Old Quarry

"They dug ten streets from that there hole," he said,
"Hard on five hundred houses." He nodded
Down the set of the quarry and spat in the water
Making a moorhen cock her head
As if a fish had leaped. "Half the new town
"Came out of yonder—King Street, Queen Street, all
"The houses round the Green as far as the slagbank,
"And Market Street, too, from the Crown allotments
"Up to the Station Yard."—"But Market Street's
"Brown freestone," I said. "Nobbut the facings;
"We called them the Khaki Houses in the Boer War,
"But they're Cumberland slate at the back."

I thought of those streets still bearing their royal names
Like the coat-of-arms on a child's Jubilee Mug—
Nonconformist gables sanded with sun
Or branded with burning creeper; a smoke of lilac
Between the blue roofs of closet and coal-house:
So much that woman's blood gave sense and shape to
Hacked from this dynamited combe.
The rocks cracked to the pond, and hawthorns fell
In waterfalls of blossom. Shed petals
Patterned the scum like studs on the sole of a boot,
And stiff-legged sparrows skid down screes of gravel.

NORMAN NICHOLSON

I saw the town's black generations
Packed in their caves of rock, as mussel or limpet
Washed by the tidal sky; then swept, shovelled
Back in the quarry again, a landslip of lintels
Blocking the gape of the tarn.
The quick turf pushed a green tarpaulin over
All that was mortal in five thousand lives.
Nor did it seem a paradox to one
Who held quarry and query, turf and town,
In the small lock of a recording brain.

HENRY REED

Judging Distances

Not only how far away, but the way that you say it
Is very important. Perhaps you may never get
The knack of judging a distance, but at least you know
How to report on a landscape: the central sector,
The right of arc and that, which we had last Tuesday,
  And at least you know

That maps are of time, not place, so far as the army
Happens to be concerned—the reason being,
Is one which need not delay us. Again, you know
There are three kinds of tree, three only, the fir and the poplar,
And those which have bushy tops to; and lastly
  That things only seem to be things.

A barn is not called a barn, to put it more plainly,
Or a field in the distance, where sheep may be safely grazing.
You must never be over-sure. You must say, when reporting:
At five o'clock in the central sector is a dozen
Of what appear to be animals; whatever you do,
  Don't call the bleeders *sheep*.

I am sure that's quite clear; and suppose, for the sake of
   example,
The one at the end, asleep, endeavours to tell us
What he sees over there to the west, and how far away,
After first having come to attention. There to the west,
On the fields of summer the sun and the shadows bestow
   Vestments of purple and gold.

The still white dwellings are like a mirage in the heat,
And under the swaying elms a man and a woman
Lie gently together. Which is, perhaps, only to say
That there is a row of houses to the left of arc,
And that under some poplars a pair of what appear to be humans
   Appear to be loving.

Well that, for an answer, is what we might rightly call
Moderately satisfactory only, the reason being,
Is that two things have been omitted, and those are important.
The human beings, now: in what direction are they,
And how far away, would you say? And do not forget
   There may be dead ground in between.

There may be dead ground in between; and I may not have got
The knack of judging a distance; I will only venture
A guess that perhaps between me and the apparent lovers,
(Who, incidentally, appear by now to have finished,)
At seven o'clock from the houses, is roughly a distance
   Of about one year and a half.

A Map of Verona

*Quelle belle heure, quels bons bras me
rendront ces régions d'où viennent mes
sommeils et mes moindres mouvements?*

A map of Verona is open, the small strange city;
With its river running round and through, it is river-embraced,
And over this city for a whole long winter season,
Through streets on a map, my thoughts have hovered and paced.

Across the river there is a wandering suburb,
An unsolved smile on a now familiar mouth;
Some enchantments of earlier towns are about you:
Once I was drawn to Naples in the south.

Naples I know now, street and hovel and garden,
The look of the islands from the avenue,
Capri and Ischia, like approaching drum-beats—
My youthful Naples, how I remember you!

You were an early chapter, a practice in sorrow,
Your shadows fell, but were only a token of pain,
A sketch in tenderness, lust, and sudden parting,
And I shall not need to trouble with you again.

But I remember, once your map lay open,
As now Verona's, under the still lamp-light.
I thought, are these the streets to walk in in the mornings,
Are these the gardens to linger in at night?

And all was useless that I thought I learned:
Maps are of place, not time, nor can they say
The surprising height and colour of a building,
Nor where the groups of people bar the way.

It is strange to remember those thoughts and to try to catch
The underground whispers of music beneath the years,
The forgotten conjectures, the clouded, forgotten vision,
Which only in vanishing phrases reappears.

Again, it is strange to lead a conversation
Round to a name, to a cautious questioning
Of travellers, who talk of Juliet's tomb and fountains
And a shining smile of snowfall, late in Spring.

Their memories calm this winter of expectation,
Their talk restrains me, for I cannot flow
Like your impetuous river to embrace you;
Yet you are there, and one day I shall go.

234

HENRY REED

The train will bring me perhaps in utter darkness
And drop me where you are blooming, unaware
That a stranger has entered your gates, and a new devotion
Is about to attend and haunt you everywhere.

The flutes are warm: in tomorrow's cave the music
Trembles and forms inside the musician's mind,
The lights begin, and the shifting crowds in the causeways
Are discerned through the dusk, and the rolling river behind.

And in what hour of beauty, in what good arms,
Shall I those regions and that city attain
From whence my dreams and slightest movements rise?
And what good Arms shall take them away again?

DYLAN THOMAS

Especially when the October wind

Especially when the October wind
With frosty fingers punishes my hair,
Caught by the crabbing sun I walk on fire
And cast a shadow crab upon the land,
By the sea's side, hearing the noise of birds,
Hearing the raven cough in winter sticks,
My busy heart who shudders as she talks
Sheds the syllabic blood and drains her words.

Shut, too, in a tower of words, I mark
On the horizon walking like the trees
The wordy shapes of women, and the rows
Of the star-gestured children in the park.
Some let me make you of the vowelled beeches,
Some of the oaken voices, from the roots
Of many a thorny shire tell you notes,
Some let me make you of the water's speeches.

235

Behind a pot of ferns the wagging clock
Tells me the hour's word, the neural meaning
Flies on the shafted disk, declaims the morning
And tells the windy weather in the cock.
Some let me make you of the meadow's signs;
The signal grass that tells me all I know
Breaks with the wormy winter through the eye.
Some let me tell you of the raven's sins.

Especially when the October wind
(Some let me make you of autumnal spells,
The spider-tongued, and the loud hill of Wales)
With fists of turnips punishes the land,
Some let me make you of the heartless words.
The heart is drained that, spelling in the scurry
Of chemic blood, warned of the coming fury.
By the sea's side hear the dark-vowelled birds.

And death shall have no dominion

And death shall have no dominion.
Dead men naked they shall be one
With the man in the wind and the west moon;
When their bones are picked clean and the clean
    bones gone,
They shall have stars at elbow and foot;
Though they go mad they shall be sane,
Though they sink through the sea they shall rise
    again;
Though lovers be lost love shall not;
And death shall have no dominion.

And death shall have no dominion.
Under the windings of the sea
They lying long shall not die windily;
Twisting on racks when sinews give way,
Strapped to a wheel, yet they shall not break;

Faith in their hands shall snap in two,
And the unicorn evils run them through;
Split all ends up they shan't crack;
And death shall have no dominion.

And death shall have no dominion.
No more may gulls cry at their ears
Or waves break loud on the seashores;
Where blew a flower may a flower no more
Lift its head to the blows of the rain;
Though they be mad and dead as nails,
Heads of the characters hammer through daisies;
Break in the sun till the sun breaks down,
And death shall have no dominion.

A Refusal to Mourn the Death, by Fire, of a Child in London

Never until the mankind making
Bird beast and flower
Fathering and all humbling darkness
Tells with silence the last light breaking
And the still hour
Is come of the sea tumbling in harness

And I must enter again the round
Zion of the water bead
And the synagogue of the ear of corn
Shall I let pray the shadow of a sound
Or sow my salt seed
In the least valley of sackcloth to mourn

The majesty and burning of the child's death.
I shall not murder
The mankind of her going with a grave truth
Nor blaspheme down the stations of the breath
With any further
Elegy of innocence and youth.

Deep with the first dead lies London's daughter,
Robed in the long friends,
The grains beyond age, the dark veins of her
    mother,
Secret by the unmourning water
Of the riding Thames.
After the first death, there is no other.

Do not go gentle into that good night

Do not go gentle into that good night,
Old age should burn and rave at close of day;
Rage, rage against the dying of the light.

Though wise men at their end know dark is right,
Because their words have forked no lightning they
Do not go gentle into that good night.

Good men, the last wave by, crying how bright
Their frail deeds might have danced in a green bay,
Rage, rage against the dying of the light.

Wild men who caught and sang the sun in flight,
And learn, too late, they grieved it on its way,
Do not go gentle into that good night.

Grave men, near death, who see with blinding sight
Blind eyes could blaze like meteors and be gay,
Rage, rage against the dying of the light.

And you, my father, there on the sad height,
Curse, bless, me now with your fierce tears, I pray.
Do not go gentle into that good night.
Rage, rage against the dying of the light.

DYLAN THOMAS

In My Craft or Sullen Art

In my craft or sullen art
Exercised in the still night
When only the moon rages
And the lovers lie abed
With all their griefs in their arms,
I labour by singing light
Not for ambition or bread
Or the strut and trade of charms
On the ivory stages
But for the common wages
Of their most secret heart.

Not for the proud man apart
From the raging moon I write
On these spindrift pages
Nor for the towering dead
With their nightingales and psalms
But for the lovers, their arms
Round the griefs of the ages,
Who pay no praise or wages
Nor heed my craft or art.

Fern Hill

Now as I was young and easy under the apple boughs
About the lilting house and happy as the grass was green,
   The night above the dingle starry,
    Time let me hail and climb
   Golden in the heydays of his eyes,
And honoured among wagons I was prince of the apple towns
And once below a time I lordly had the trees and leaves
    Trail with daisies and barley
  Down the rivers of the windfall light.

And as I was green and carefree, famous among the barns
About the happy yard and singing as the farm was home,
   In the sun that is young once only,
     Time let me play and be
   Golden in the mercy of his means,
And green and golden I was huntsman and herdsman, the calves
Sang to my horn, the foxes on the hills barked clear and cold,
   And the sabbath rang slowly
   In the pebbles of the holy streams.

All the sun long it was running, it was lovely, the hay
Fields high as the house, the tunes from the chimneys, it was air
   And playing, lovely and watery
     And fire green as grass.
   And nightly under the simple stars
As I rode to sleep the owls were bearing the farm away,
All the moon long I heard, blessed among stables, the nightjars
   Flying with the ricks, and the horses
     Flashing into the dark.

And then to awake, and the farm, like a wanderer white
With the dew, come back, the cock on his shoulder: it was all
   Shining, it was Adam and maiden,
     The sky gathered again
   And the sun grew round that very day.
So it must have been after the birth of the simple light
In the first, spinning place, the spellbound horses walking warm
   Out of the whinnying green stable
     On to the fields of praise.

And honoured among foxes and pheasants by the gay house
Under the new made clouds and happy as the heart was long,
   In the sun born over and over,
     I ran my heedless ways,
   My wishes raced through the house high hay
And nothing I cared, at my sky blue trades, that time allows
In all his tuneful turning so few and such morning songs
   Before the children green and golden
     Follow him out of grace,

DYLAN THOMAS

Nothing I cared, in the lamb white days, that time would take me
Up to the swallow thronged loft by the shadow of my hand,
  In the moon that is always rising,
    Nor that riding to sleep
  I should hear him fly with the high fields
And wake to the farm forever fled from the childless land.
Oh as I was young and easy in the mercy of his means,
    Time held me green and dying
  Though I sang in my chains like the sea.

PETER YATES

Star of Eternal Possibles and Joy

Star of eternal possibles and joy,
Vibrate the marble with your kiss!
On ancient columns and dark walls
  Fall with unearthly calls,
Bird-supple wings disturbing air!

Fall like the rain on praying hands;
Bring to the living-haunted hills
Remote perspectives and new worlds—
  Invasion of the wilds,
Illumination of nocturnal fairs.

Disturb the logic of bleak winds—
Rotations of the mind unwinding life;
And in the midnight waiting groves,
  The ever-talking graves
Crying aloud the perfect word.

Aim for the fringe, the thinnest curve
Where strength of possible despairs:
The missing but imagined arc
  For which the circle aches,
The vista waiting to be seen.

I breaking from the ring of we,
Cries in its isolation still:
A leap from sequence into void!
    But in that daring vague
The ether challenges with form.

O star of mind's dark inwardness,
Prolong the struggle with your force!
By your not-being dare to be
    More than the eye can see:
A silence audible with growth.

Thought and the Poet

Incorrigible one, still groping with your eyes
Inflamed, in strange bewilderment of living now,
Can you stir up, from pools reflecting sombre skies
Fresh images? unwrinkle being from the brow,
And light as happiness, instinctive as the birds
Pick the world's rubble for your fascinating words?

Truth casts down, yet poetry must still engender
Animal senses from the smell of human pain.
In Easter gaiety branches burst their tender
Emerald buds, and pavements glint with April rain.
But always, blowing grit into God's perfect eye
Thought tempts the animal senses, and they lie.

In such despair, some say, man's shape misshapen grows,
While twanging overhead, shot from the supple trees
Birds' arrows fly, and Spring's green whistle thoughtless blows.
Look for the images of human song in these!
But are men birds, or blossoms exquisitely curled?
We think, and thought corrupts love's image of the world.

242

PETER YATES

Smelling the End of Green July

Smelling the end of green July
I entered through spiked-gates a London park
To grill my body in the sun,
And to untie thought's parcel of pure dark
Under the blue gaze of the candid sky.

The air was heavy, without breath;
The asphalt paths gave off a hollow ring;
And wearing haloes of shrill birds
The statues watched the flowers withering,
And leaves curl up for Summer's rusty death.

O zoo-like sameness of all parks!
The grasses lick the railings of wrought-iron,
And chains clink in the shrubbery
As Summer roaring like a shabby lion
Claws at the meaning of the human marks.

I saw the tops of buses wheel
Geranium flashes over pigeon-walls;
And heard the rocket-cries of children
Fly upwards, bursting where the water calls,
And scissors sunlight with a glint of steel.

The wings of slowly dripping light
Pulled boats across a swan-enlightened lake;
And near youth's skipping-ropes of joy
I felt the strings of my old parcel break,
Spilling its cold abstractions with delight.

I watched the games of life begun
Among dead matches, droppings of the birds;
And left thought's parcel on a bench
While I relearned the flight of singing words
Under the blowlamp kisses of the sun.

243

JOHN CORNFORD

Huesca

Heart of the heartless world,
Dear heart, the thought of you
Is the pain at my side,
The shadow that chills my view.

The wind rises in the evening,
Reminds that autumn is near.
I am afraid to lose you,
I am afraid of my fear.

On the last mile to Huesca,
The last fence for our pride,
Think so kindly, dear, that I
Sense you at my side.

And if bad luck should lay my strength
Into the shallow grave,
Remember all the good you can;
Don't forget my love.

G. S. FRASER

Song for Music

The fountains and the garden,
The garden and the ghost,
I lay my love before you
And do not count the cost
And know my love is lost.

I lay my love before you
For your unlucky hands
To break and spoil, but suffer
To suffer, while it stands,
What no one understands.

You will not break nor spoil it
Since you have other loves
Gathered with beaks as eager
Out of the air as doves
To peck your olive groves.

But suffer it to hover,
But suffer it to live,
Around the pools and fountains
Ghostly, where ghost birds dive
And both are fugitive.

Birds of the air I call you,
Birds of the air, my throng,
Towards a ghost oasis
Where I shall linger long
But longer shall my song.

When images have faded
Like this delightful tree
Of mirage, like these waters
That were not meant to be,
My song, come back to me.

Come in another country
And with another coat
To smart my eyes to sobbing
And catch me by the throat
With these things of no note.

LAURIE LEE

First Love

That was her beginning, an apparition
of rose in the unbreathed airs of his love,
her heart revealed by the wash of summer
sprung from her childhood's shallow stream.

Then it was that she put up her hair,
inscribed her eyes with a look of grief,
while her limbs grew as curious as coral branches,
her breast full of secrets.

But the boy, confused in his day's desire,
was searching for herons, his fingers bathed
in the green of walnuts, or watching at night
the Great Bear spin from the maypole star.

It was then that he paused in the death of a game,
felt the hook of her hair on his swimming throat,
saw her mouth at large in the dark river
flushed like a salmon.

But he covered his face and hid his joy
in a wild-goose web of false directions,
and hunted the woods for eggs and glow-worms,
for rabbits tasteless as moss.

And she walked in fields where the crocuses
branded her feet, where mares' tails sprang
from the prancing lake, and the salty grasses
surged round her stranded body.

Juniper

Juniper holds to the moon
a girl adoring a bracelet;
as the hills draw up their knees
they throw off their jasmine girdles.

You are a forest of game,
a thought of nights in procession,
you tread through the bitter fires
of the nasturtium.

I decorate you to a smell of apples,
I divide you among the voices
of owls and cavaliering cocks
and woodpigeons monotonously dry.

I hang lanterns on your mouth
and candles from your passionate crucifix,
and bloody leaves of the virginia
drip with their scarlet oil.

There is a pike in the lake
whose blue teeth eat the midnight stars
piercing the water's velvet skin
and puncturing your sleep.

I am the pike in your breast,
my eyes of clay revolve the waves
while cirrus roots and lilies grow
between our banks of steep embraces.

Milkmaid

The girl's far treble, muted to the heat,
calls like a fainting bird across the fields
to where her flock lies panting for her voice,
their black horns buried deep in marigolds.

They climb awake, like drowsy butterflies,
and press their red flanks through the tall branched
    grass,
and as they go their wandering tongues embrace
the vacant summer mirrored in their eyes.

Led to the limestone shadows of a barn
they snuff their past embalmèd in the hay,
while her cool hand, cupped to the udder's fount,
distils the brimming harvest of their day.

247

Look what a cloudy cream the earth gives out,
fat juice of buttercups and meadow-rye;
the girl dreams milk within her body's field
and hears, far off, her muted children cry.

Village of Winter Carols

Village of winter carols
and gawdy spinning tops,
of green-handed walnuts
and games in the moon.

You were adventure's web,
the flag of fear I flew
riding black stallions
through the rocky streets.

You were the first faint map
of the mysterious sun,
chart of my island flesh
and the mushroom-tasting kiss.

But no longer do I join
your children's sharp banditti,
nor seek the glamour of
your ravished apples.

Your hillocks build no more
their whales and pyramids,
nor howl across the night
their springing wolves.

For crouching in my brain
the crafty thigh of love
twists your old landscape
with a new device.

LAURIE LEE

And every field has grown
a strange and flowering pit
where I must try the blind
and final trick of youth.

DIANA WITHERBY

Casualty

Death stretched down two hands,
One on desert sands
Shut his eyes. The other in her head
Opened the third eye of ruin; instead
Of doubt, which veiled it, certainty now gives it sight,
Staring dark and twitching when she sleeps at night,
When she wakes turning her, indifferent, from light.

Sometimes looking through a door into a sunny room, cold,
Full of furniture, but empty except for herself, old
In the mirror. Sometimes resting on fields flowing their green gold
Flowers, giving her an illusion of summer, but her thawing tear
Freezes quickly in the eternal ice of confirmed fear.
Sometimes, drifting along the canal of fatigue, he seems near,
The eye is closing—then suddenly starts in her brain,
Opens—He is gone. She, with walls, iron-coloured rain,
Railings silhouetted either side, is alone again.

We, who for our own comfort, imagined that a grief,
Could be smoothed and stroked by time to its relief,
Looking at her face, know now that only their brief
Past stands. The sun has equal entrance there
With mist or wind. We move in talking where
Gates stood—but voices fade,
Transfixed, in her stone shade.

DAVID GASCOYNE

Winter Garden

The season's anguish, crashing whirlwind, ice,
Have passed, and cleansed the trodden paths
That silent gardeners have strewn with ash.

The iron circles of the sky
Are worn away by tempest;
Yet in this garden there is no more strife:
The Winter's knife is buried in the earth.
Pure music is the cry that tears
The birdless branches in the wind.
No blossom is reborn. The blue
Stare of the pond is blind.

And no-one sees
A restless stranger through the morning stray
Across the sodden lawn, whose eyes
Are tired of weeping, in whose breast
A savage sun consumes its hidden day.

Ecce Homo

Whose is this horrifying face,
This putrid flesh, discoloured, flayed,
Fed on by flies, scorched by the sun?
Whose are these hollow red-filmed eyes
And thorn-spiked head and spear-stuck side?
Behold the Man: he is Man's Son.

Forget the legend, tear the decent veil
That cowardice or interest devised
To make their mortal enemy a friend,
To hide the bitter truth all His wounds tell,
Lest the great scandal be no more disguised:
He is in agony till the world's end,

And we must never sleep during that time!
He is suspended on the cross-tree now
And we are onlookers at the crime,
Callous contemporaries of the slow
Torture of God. Here is the hill
Made ghastly by His spattered blood

Whereon he hangs and suffers still:
See, the centurions wear riding-boots,
Black shirts and badges and peaked caps,
Greet one another with raised-arm salutes;
They have cold eyes, unsmiling lips;
Yet these His brothers know not what they do.

And on His either side hang dead
A labourer and a factory hand,
Or one is maybe a lynched Jew
And one a Negro or a Red,
Coolie or Ethiopian, Irishman,
Spaniard or German democrat.

Behind His lolling head the sky
Glares like a fiery cataract
Red with the murders of two thousand years
Committed in His name and by
Crusaders, Christian warriors
Defending faith and property.

Amid the plain beneath His transfixed hands,
Exuding darkness as indelible
As guilty stains, fanned by funereal
And lurid airs, besieged by drifting sands
And clefted landslides our about-to-be
Bombed and abandoned cities stand.

DAVID GASCOYNE

He who wept for Jerusalem
Now sees His prophecy extend
Across the greatest cities of the world,
A guilty panic reason cannot stem
Rising to raze them all as He foretold;
And He must watch this drama to the end.

Though often named, He is unknown
To the dark kingdoms at His feet
Where everything disparages His words,
And each man bears the common guilt alone
And goes blindfolded to his fate,
And fear and greed are sovereign lords.

The turning point of history
Must come. Yet the complacent and the proud
And who exploit and kill, may be denied—
Christ of Revolution and of Poetry—
The resurrection and the life
Wrought by your·spirit's blood.

Involved in their own sophistry
The black priest and the upright man
Faced by subversive truth shall be struck dumb,
Christ of Revolution and of Poetry,
While the rejected and condemned become
Agents of the divine.

Not from a monstrance silver-wrought
But from the tree of human pain
Redeem our sterile misery,
Christ of Revolution and of Poetry,
That man's long journey through the night
May not have been in vain.

DAVID GASCOYNE

Apologia

Poète et non honnête homme
PASCAL

I

It's not the age,
Disease, or accident, but sheer
Perversity (or so one must suppose),
That pins me to the singularly bare
Boards of this trestle-stage
That I have mounted to adopt the pose
Of a demented wrestler, with gorge full
Of phlegm, eyes bleared with salt, and knees
Knocking like ninepins: a most furious fool!

2

Fixed by the nib
Of an inept pen to a bleak page
Before the glassy gaze of a ghost mob,
I stand once more to face the silent rage
Of my unseen Opponent, and begin
The same old struggle for the doubtful prize:
Each stanza is a round, and every line
A blow aimed at the too elusive chin
Of that Oblivion which cannot fail to win.

3

Before I fall
Down silent finally, I want to make
One last attempt at utterance, and tell
How my absurd desire was to compose
A single poem with my mental eyes
Wide open, and without even one lapse
From that most scrupulous Truth which I pursue
When not pursuing Poetry.—Perhaps
Only the poem I can never write is *true*.

253

DAVID GASCOYNE

Rex Mundi

I heard a herald's note announce the coming of a king.

He who came sounding his approach was a small boy;
The household trumpet that he flourished a tin toy.

Then from a bench beneath the boughs that lately Spring
Had hung again with green across the avenue, I rose
To render to the king who came the homage subjects owe.

And as I waited, wondered why it was that such a few
Were standing there with me to see him pass; but understood
As soon as he came into sight, this was a monarch no
Crowds of this world can recognize, to hail him as they should.

He drove past in a carriage that was drawn by a white goat:
King of the world to come where all that shall be now is new,
Calmly he gazed on our pretentious present that is not.

Of morals, classes, business, war, this child
Knew nothing. We were pardoned when he smiled.

If you hear it in the distance, do not scorn the herald's note.

JACK R. CLEMO

The Water-Wheel

Dead wood with its load of stones
    Amid the living wood!
Tugged by the wheel the ballast groans,
    Casts on the little brood
    Of trees its alien mood.

The wheel spins dourly round,
  Wet flanges menacing,
Yet curbed and forced back underground,
  Snarling and shuddering
  Beneath the water's sting.

The iron rods are gripped;
  Tree-high the pulleys slur:
The budding boughs are bruised and stripped:
  Dead iron, live branches blur
  In rhythmic massacre.

The plashy ground turns white
  With clay-silt from the wheel,
And still the trough pours on to smite
  Both wood and iron, to seal
  The dream-world with the real.

A Calvinist in Love

I will not kiss you country fashion,
  By hedgesides where
  Weasel and hare
Claim kinship with our passion.

I care no more for fickle moonlight:
  Would rather see
  Your face touch me
Under a claywork dune-light.

I want no scent or softness round us
  When we embrace:
  We could not trace
Therein what beauties bound us.

This bare clay-pit is truest setting
  For love like ours:
  No bed of flowers
But sand-ledge for our petting.

The Spring is not our mating season:
   The lift of sap
   Would but entrap
Our souls and lead to treason.

This truculent gale, this pang of winter
   Awake our joy,
   For they employ
Moods that made Calvary splinter.

We need no vague and dreamy fancies:
   Care not to sight
   The Infinite
In transient necromancies.

No poetry of earth can fasten
   Its vampire mouth
   Upon our youth:
We know the sly assassin.

We cannot fuse with fallen Nature's
   Our rhythmic tide:
   It is allied
With laws beyond the creatures.

It draws from older, sterner oceans
   Its sensuous swell:
   Too near to Hell
Are we for earthly motions.

Our love is full-grown Dogma's offspring,
   Election's child,
   Making the wild
Heats of our blood an offering.

ALUN LEWIS

Song

(On seeing dead bodies floating off the Cape)

The first months of his absence
I was numb and sick
And where he'd left his promise
Life did not turn or kick.
The seed, the seed of love was sick.

The second month my eyes were sunk
In the darkness of despair,
And my bed was like a grave
And his ghost was lying there.
And my heart was sick with care.

The third month of his going
I thought I heard him say
"Our course deflected slightly
On the thirty-second day—"
The tempest blew his words away.

And he was lost among the waves,
His ship rolled helpless in the sea
The fourth month of his voyage
He shouted grievously
"Beloved do not think of me."

The flying fish like kingfishers
Skim the sea's bewildered crests,
The whales blow steaming fountains,
The seagulls have no nests
Where my lover sways and rests.

We never thought to buy and sell
This life that blooms or withers in the leaf,
And I'll not stir, so he sleeps well,
Though cell by cell the coral reef
Builds an eternity of grief.

But oh! the drag and dullness of my Self;
The turning seasons wither in my head;
All this slowness, all this hardness,
The nearness that is waiting in my bed,
The gradual self-effacement of the dead.

Water Music

Deep in the heart of the lake
Where the last light is clinging
A strange foreboding voice
Is patiently singing.

Do not fear to venture
Where the last light trembles
Because you were in love.
Love never dissembles.

Fear no more the boast, the bully,
The lies, the vain labour.
Make no show for death
As for a rich neighbour.

What stays of the great religions?
An old priest, an old birth.
What stays of the great battles?
Dust on the earth.

Cold is the lake water
And dark as history.
Hurry not and fear not
This oldest mystery.

This strange voice singing,
This slow deep drag of the lake,
This yearning, yearning, this ending
Of the heart and its ache.

ALUN LEWIS

Bivouac

There was no trace of Heaven
That night as we lay
Punch-drunk and blistered with sunlight
On the ploughed-up clay.

I remembered the cactus where our wheels
Had bruised it, bleeding white;
And a fat rat crouching beadyeyed
Caught by my light;

And the dry disturbing whispers
Of the agitated wood,
With its leathery vendetta,
Mantillas dark with blood.

And the darkness drenched with Evil
Haunting as a country song,
Ignoring the protesting cry
Of Right and Wrong.

Yet the peasant was drawing water
With the first excited bird
And the dawn with childish eyes
Observed us as we stirred

And the milk-white oxen waited
Docile at the yoke
As we clipped on our equipment
And scarcely spoke

Being bewildered by the night
And only aware
Of the withering obsession
That lovers grow to fear
When the last note is written
And at last and alone
One of them wakes in terror
And the other is gone.

TERENCE TILLER

Bathers

They flutter out of white, and run
through the electric wind to bathe,
giggling like rivers for the fun
of smacking mud in the toes, of lithe
and sliding bodies like their own
—sharp rushes, good to battle with.

The child knows all delight to be
naked and queer as his own name,
foreign as being loved; but he
feels as a kind of coming home
the flags that slap his plunging knee,
and the cold stocking of the stream.

Coiling in wombs of water, bent
backwards upon the sheets of air,
his wand of sexless body lent
to all that was or casts before,
he strips to either element
a foetus or a ravisher.

So gladly virgin rivers rush
down to their amniotic seas,
children of cold and glittering flesh
that promise harvest as they pass
panics of tiny fertile fish
in the fast pale of boisterous thighs.

The End of the Story

Put out the candle, close the biting rose,
for cock and cony are asleep; the sheep
in her secretive hills, with fleece at peace,
now lies enfolded.

The hungry sceptre-kissing mouth, the moth
behind the fingers, no more eat the night;
the rooting worm has crawled away from play
in his wet burrows.

Now the extremest joys are dreams and toys;
it's darkness in a vast full-tide abed;
over abandoned bodies time shall climb
like the black spider.

Give memory all amazing hours, all showers
or sharply pouring seas between the knees;
slack as a rope, the flesh is dull, and full
of its perfection.

And all that lately flashed and leapt is gripped
into a knot of symbols; all's grown small,
quiet as curtains: brave be this your grave,
and fresh your garlands.

The Vase

Slowly the roses bleed into the water,
a wound, a garlanded mouth, in every stem;
a languid sweetness turning rich and bitter
—the last of Rome.

Fragile and wistful as the weather, caught
naked and cold in flowers, with the grace
of virgin dancers, is the apricot
in our blue glass.

Barbarian slaves: the grounds where roses grow
are wild and thorny in their flaunting weeds;
where, stripped for wind, the flowering trees bow to
their green brides.

TERENCE TILLER

Oh trees in your arms lulling the wind;
roses written by the sun your open lips:
to what imperial splendour are you bound,
and by what steps?

Crushed in the beauty and the liquid noose,
you dance the apricot, draw the slow breath
of roses dying like Petronius
a seemly death.

CHARLES CAUSLEY

On Seeing a Poet of the First World War on the Station at Abbeville

Poet, cast your careful eye
Where the beached songs of summer lie,
  White fell the wave that splintered
  The wreck where once you wintered,
White as the snows that lair
Your freezing hair.

Captain, here you took your wine,
The trees at ease in the orchard-line,
  Bonny the errand-boy bird
  Whistles the songs you once heard,
While you traverse the wire,
Autumn will hold her fire.

Through the tall wood the thunder ran
As when the gibbering guns began,
  Swift as a murderer by the stack
  Crawled the canal with fingers black,
Black with your brilliant blood
You lit the mud.

CHARLES CAUSLEY

Two grey moths stare from your eyes,
Sharp is your sad face with surprise.
   In the stirring pool I fail
    To see the drowned of Passchendaele,
Where all day drives for me
The spoiling sea.

W. S. GRAHAM

Letter VI

A day the wind was hardly
Shaking the youngest frond
Of April I went on
The high moor we know.
I put my childhood out
Into a cocked hat
And you moving the myrtle
Walked slowly over.
A sweet clearness became.
The Clyde sleeved in its firth
Reached and dazzled me.
I moved and caught the sweet
Courtesy of your mouth.
My breath to your breath.
And as you lay fondly
In the crushed smell of the moor
The courageous and just sun
Opened its door.
And there we lay halfway
Your body and my body
On the high moor. Without
A word then we went
Our ways. I heard the moor
Curling its cries far
Across the still loch.
The great verbs of the sea
Come down on us in a roar.
What shall I answer for?

JOHN HEATH-STUBBS

Address Not Known

So you are gone, and are proved bad change, as we had always
   known,
And I am left lonely in London the metropolitan city,
Perhaps to twist this incident into a durable poem—
The lesson of those who give their love to phenomenal beauty.

I am coming to think now that all I have loved were shadows
Strayed up from a dead world, through a gap in a raped tomb,
Or where the narcissus battens in mythological meadows:
Your face was painted upon the coffin-lid from Fayoum.

Is this my pain that is speaking? The pain was not long
   protracted:
I make a statement, forgive the betrayal, the meanness, the theft.
Human, I cannot suppose you had planned all that was enacted:
Fortitude must be procured to encounter the hollowness left.

The sun will not haver in its course for the lack of you,
Nor the flowers fail in colour, nor the bird stint in its song.
Only the heart that wanted somehow to have opened up
Finds the frost in the day's air, and the nights which appear too
   long.

JAMES KIRKUP

A Correct Compassion

To Mr. Philip Allison, after watching him perform a Mitral
Stenosis Valvulotomy in the General Infirmary at Leeds.

Cleanly, sir, you went to the core of the matter.
Using the purest kind of wit, a balance of belief and art,
You with a curious nervous elegance laid bare
The root of life, and put your finger on its beating heart.

The glistening theatre swarms with eyes, and hands, and eyes.
On green-clothed tables, ranks of instruments transmit a sterile
    gleam.
The masks are on, and no unnecessary smile betrays
A certain tension, true concomitant of calm.

Here we communicate by looks, though words,
Too, are used, as in continuous historic present
You describe our observations and your deeds.
All gesture is reduced to its result, an instrument.

She who does not know she is a patient lies
Within a tent of green, and sleeps without a sound
Beneath the lamps, and the reflectors that devise
Illuminations probing the profoundest wound.

A calligraphic master, improvising, you invent
The first incision, and no poet's hesitation
Before his snow-blank page mars your intent:
The flowing stroke is drawn like an uncalculated inspiration.

A garland of flowers unfurls across the painted flesh.
With quick precision the arterial forceps click.
Yellow threads are knotted with a simple flourish.
Transfused, the blood preserves its rose, though it is sick.

Meters record the blood, measure heart-beats, control the
    breath.
Hieratic gesture: scalpel bares a creamy rib; with pincer knives
The bone quietly is clipped, and lifted out. Beneath,
The pink, black-mottled lung like a revolted creature heaves,

Collapses; as if by extra fingers is neatly held aside
By two ordinary egg-beaters, kitchen tools that curve
Like extraordinary hands. Heart, laid bare, silently beats. It can
    hide
No longer yet is not revealed.—"A local anaesthetic in the
    cardiac nerve."

Now, in firm hands that quiver with a careful strength,
Your knife feels through the heart's transparent skin; at first,
Inside the pericardium, slit down half its length,
The heart, black-veined, swells like a fruit about to burst,

But goes on beating, love's poignant image bleeding at the dart
Of a more grievous passion, as a bird, dreaming of flight, sleeps
    on
Within its leafy cage.—"It generally upsets the heart
A bit, though not unduly, when I make the first injection."

Still, still the patient sleeps, and still the speaking heart is dumb.
The watchers breathe an air far sweeter, rarer than the room's.
The cold walls listen. Each in his own blood hears the drum
She hears, tented in green, unfathomable calms.

"I make a purse-string suture here, with a reserve
Suture, which I must make first, and deeper,
As a safeguard, should the other burst. In the cardiac nerve
I inject again a local anaesthetic. Could we have fresh towels to
    cover

All these adventitious ones. Now can you all see.
When I put my finger inside the valve, there may be a lot
Of blood, and it may come with quite a bang. But I let it flow,
In case there are any clots, to give the heart a good clean-out.

Now can you give me every bit of light you've got."
We stand on the benches, peering over his shoulder.
The lamp's intensest rays are concentrated on an inmost heart.
Someone coughs. "If you have to cough, you will do it outside
    this theatre."—"Yes, sir."

"How's she breathing, Doug.? Do you feel quite happy?"—
    "Yes, fairly
Happy."—"Now. I am putting my finger in the opening of the
    valve.
I can only get the tip of my finger in.—It's gradually
    Giving way.—I'm inside.—No clots.—I can feel the valve

Breathing freely now around my finger, and the heart working.
Not too much blood. It opened very nicely.
I should say that anatomically speaking
This is a perfect case.—Anatomically.

For of course, anatomy is not physiology."
We find we breathe again, and hear the surgeon hum.
Outside, in the street, a car starts up. The heart regularly
Thunders.—"I do not stitch up the pericardium.

It is not necessary."—For this is imagination's other place,
Where only necessary things are done, with the supreme and
    grave
Dexterity that ignores technique; with proper grace
Informing a correct compassion, that performs its love, and makes
    it live.

KEITH DOUGLAS

The Sea Bird

Walking along beside the beach
where the Mediterranean turns in sleep
under the cliff's demiarch

through a curtain of thought I see
a dead bird and a live bird
the dead eyeless, but with a bright eye

the live bird discovered me
and stepped from a black rock into the air—
I turn from the dead bird to watch him fly,

electric, brilliant blue,
beneath he is orange, like flame,
colours I can't believe are so,

as legendary flowers bloom
incendiary in tint, so swift he
searches about the sky for room,

towering like the cliffs of this coast
with his stiletto wing
and orange on his breast:

he has consumed and drained
the colours of the sea
and the yellow of this tidal ground

till he escapes the eye, or is a ghost
and in a moment has come down
crept into the dead bird, ceased to exist.

How to Kill

Under the parabola of a ball,
a child turning into a man,
I looked into the air too long.
The ball fell in my hand, it sang
in the closed fist: *Open Open
Behold a gift designed to kill.*

Now in my dial of glass appears
the soldier who is going to die.
He smiles, and moves about in ways
his mother knows, habits of his.
The wires touch his face: I cry
NOW. Death, like a familiar, hears

and look, has made a man of dust
of a man of flesh. This sorcery
I do. Being damned, I am amused
to see the centre of love diffused
and the waves of love travel into vacancy
How easy it is to make a ghost.

The weightless mosquito touches
her tiny shadow on the stone,
and with how like, how infinite
a lightness, man and shadow meet.
They fuse. A shadow is a man
when the mosquito death approaches.

Vergissmeinnicht

Three weeks gone and the combatants gone,
returning over the nightmare ground
we found the place again, and found
the soldier sprawling in the sun.

The frowning barrel of his gun
overshadowing. As we came on
that day, he hit my tank with one
like the entry of a demon.

Look. Here in the gunpit spoil
the dishonoured picture of his girl
who has put: *Steffi. Vergissmeinnicht*
in a copybook gothic script.

We see him almost with content
abased, and seeming to have paid
and mocked at by his own equipment
that's hard and good when he's decayed.

But she would weep to see to-day
how on his skin the swart flies move;
the dust upon the paper eye
and the burst stomach like a cave.

For here the lover and killer are mingled
who had one body and one heart.
And death who had the soldier singled
has done the lover mortal hurt.

J. C. HALL

Montgomery

Ambiguous Time, I heard you sighing
  In a small dry wind one summer's day,
As under Montgomery castle lying
  I listened to lonely ghosts astray
    Hither and thither crying.

How lost those antique voices were,
  How lost! It seemed their whispered breath
Caused scarcely a ripple on the air
  As to and fro they wandered. Death
    Seemed unremembered there.

And unremembered, too, the powers
  By which death brought those subjects low:
The ugly block, the fearful towers.
  Majesty rampant long ago,
    Now silent under flowers.

O mineral noon, despite those shades,
  Your sap gushed green in every tree;
The present flooded hill and glade
  With a fierce natural energy
    No envious past forbade.

And only I, a mortal lying
  In Time beneath those crumbling stones,
Heard in the living air the vying
  Dead, all day with ghostly moans
    Hither and thither crying.

HAMISH HENDERSON

First Elegy

There are many dead in the brutish desert,
    who lie uneasy
among the scrub in this landscape of half-wit
stunted ill-will. For the dead land is insatiate
and necrophilous. The sand is blowing about still.
Many who for various reasons, or because
    of mere unanswerable compulsion, came here
and fought among the clutching gravestones,
    shivered and sweated,
cried out, suffered thirst, were stoically silent, cursed
the spittering machine-guns, were homesick for Europe
and fast embedded in quicksand of Africa
    agonized and died.
And sleep now. Sleep here the sleep of the dust.

There were our own, there were the others.
Their deaths were like their lives, human and animal.
There were no gods and precious few heroes.
What they regretted when they died had nothing to do with
    race and leader, realm indivisible,
laboured Augustan speeches or vague imperial heritage.
(They saw through that guff before the axe fell.)
    Their longing turned to
the lost world glimpsed in the memory of letters:
an evening at the pictures in the friendly dark,
two knowing conspirators smiling and whispering secrets;
    or else
a family gathering in the homely kitchen
with Mum so proud of her boys in uniform:
    their thoughts trembled
between moments of estrangement, and ecstatic moments
of reconciliation: and their desire
crucified itself against the unutterable shadow of someone
whose photo was in their wallets.
Then death made his incision.

HAMISH HENDERSON

There were our own, there were the others.
Therefore, minding the great word of Glencoe's
son, that we should not disfigure ourselves
with villainy of hatred; and seeing that all
have gone down like curs into anonymous silence,
I will bear witness for I knew the others.
Seeing that littoral and interior are alike indifferent
And the birds are drawn again to our welcoming north
Why should I not sing *them*, the dead, the innocent?

DAVID WRIGHT

Moral Story II

I met Poetry, an old prostitute walking
Along Piccadilly, one whom no one would buy,
Just a draggletail bitch with padding for each breast,—
No wonder the corner boys were gay and joking!
She'd laid on paint too thick in a colour too high,
And scuttled like a red hen deprived of its nest.

But she stopped for a word with me, one of her pimps,
Her faithful old ponce still hoping for his percent.
When I asked, "How's business?" she shook her leary head:
"In peacetime the boys are not so keen on the nymphs;
And I'm getting a bit behind with the rent.
These days the pickings are small that fall from my bed.

"Wartime was whoretime! Never mind, cheer up, lovey;
Find me another fee like the one from New York:
They pay very nicely, the Yanks—and don't look glum.
—Or go get another girl, if you want more gravy!"
She screamed, "—you've got your good looks yet,—or you
   could work!
"Go get yourself a job licking somebody's bum!"

272

But out of the corner of my eye I'd seen a Rolls Royce
Purr by us with a back seat full of her old friends,
Passing, like the gent in the song, the girl they'd ruined.
They lifted a disdainful nostril at her noise,
And continued as you might expect, to pursue their ends,
With cigars drawing, and the radio carefully tuned

To a highbrow programme. So across the gutter
We caught one another's look; and as their exhaust
Echoed outside the Ritz like a burst paper bag,
Laughed like hyenas; she, with a shaking udder,
Said, "I was a lovely piece, when they met me first!"
And lineaments of desire lit the old hag.

SIDNEY KEYES

The Gardener

If you will come on such a day
As this, between the pink and yellow lines
Of parrot-tulips, I will be your lover.
My boots flash as they beat the silly gravel.
O come, this is your day.

Were you to lay your hand like a veined leaf
Upon my square-cut hand, I would caress
The shape of it, and that would be enough.
I note the greenfly working on the rose.
Time slips between my fingers like a leaf.

Do you resemble the silent pale-eyed angels
That follow children? Is your face a flower?
The lovers and the beggars leave the park—
And still you will not come. The gates are closing.

O it is terrible to dream of angels.

273

SIDNEY KEYES

William Wordsworth

No room for mourning: he's gone out
Into the noisy glen, or stands between the stones
Of the gaunt ridge, or you'll hear his shout
Rolling among the screes, he being a boy again.
He'll never fail nor die
And if they laid his bones
In the wet vaults or iron sarcophagi
Of fame, he'd rise at the first summer rain
And stride across the hills to seek
His rest among the broken lands and clouds.
He was a stormy day, a granite peak
Spearing the sky; and look, about its base
Words flower like crocuses in the hanging woods,
Blank though the dalehead and the bony face.

ALAN ROSS

Leave Train

Yellow as flowers as dead fingers
Yellow as death as a mandarin
Dawn with eyes like a stranger
Dawn with a handful of sick flowers.

The stumps of memory are broken trees
The stumps of memory are amputated fingers
The patient sick with ether
Dreams unflowered avenues of anger.

Grief clenched like a fist, a
Sprawled hand, grief pitted with shell.
The bell of the blood in a deep sea
Drowns, the hood of the face is eyeless.

ALAN ROSS

Dawn constellated with sick stars
Dawn hedged round with smoke
Yellow as fog as cornflowers
Yellow as a dog as a death's head.

Like dissevered arteries and veins
Like brains cauterised and eyes
Protuberant with grief, the staring
Unbelief writhes bloodshot

In the tearless lids. The massed weirs,
Frozen of feeling, are empty with disuse.
Without you without you without you
Branches like nerves are sporadic with fever.

Yellow as dead flowers as a remembered South
Yellow as desire as face to face
Dawn with a handful of unnecessary hours
Dawn with cut flowers and a mouth of disaster.

HELEN SPALDING

The Dream

That evening, when the fire was lit,
She threw a cushion on the floor
Beside his chair; she liked to sit
There at his feet.

"I had a dream last night," she said,
Gazing into the friendly fire.
"I stood outside a certain door
Knowing that I would come to harm.

I slowly opened it, and saw
A small white room.
There was a man behind the door,
Standing upon a chair; his head
Shone honey-gold; he raised his arm
And slit my throat. I fell down dead."

She laughed. "The curious things we do
In dreams. I felt along my throat,
Trying to tidy it. I knew
That I was dead, so laid my coat
Over my head, because the sight
Was ugly and the floor was white.

"It seemed so lonely, then; so still;
And there was none to pity me.
I longed for pity; longed to tell
How I had died. I thought, Maybe
Someone will bring a coffin soon,
And lay me in it tenderly,
And close my eyes and mourn for me.

"Oh, how I longed for that! Some friend,
Some living friend, to see, and mind.
But then my desolation grew.
Why should the living condescend?
They seemed so different now, so strong,
So terrible, the ones I knew.

"I could not think that I had been
As splendid, beautiful as they.
The living were a world away
Beyond my servile whimpering.
For I was now a cringing thing,
A body that in terror lay,
A stupid thing with lolling head,
Meaningless, mutilated, dead.

"I thought, they must not see my
   shame,
Those sovereign ones. I longed to weep.
I longed to tell, but no one came.
I struggled to recall my name,
But felt the clumsy rigor creep
Into my veins and stupefy
The remnant of my useless will;
The blood that fed my brain was dry;
I could not now remember why
I was so ugly and so still.

"Minutes, hours, years—I do not know
How much of living time passed by.
But suddenly a frightened girl
Stood on the threshold of the door.
Her eyes were fixed upon the floor.

"She did not enter the white room,
Nor move her eyes, nor come to me,
But she was of the living—she
Was of the living! That alone
Gave me new power, and I could see
Through my glazed eyes, and through
   the coat
That covered up my gaping throat.

"And I could speak. I cannot tell
Whether with lips and tongue. I said
'Listen! Please listen! Have you heard
Them say on earth that living men
Sometimes hear voices from the dead?'
She could not answer me, and yet
I knew she heard and understood.
'You will remember this,' I said,
'For I am speaking, and am dead.'

HELEN SPALDING

"She did not move because of fear.
'Now you must go,' I said, 'but when
Out of your sleep you wake again,
Remember that you saw me here,
And tell the ones I loved.' And then
She must have woken from her sleep
Because I watched the darkness creep
Across the door, across the room,
And seal my tomb."

She finished, and smiled up at him.
She shivered, but she was not cold.
In the bright circle of the lamp
His head shone honey-gold.

NORMAN MacCAIG

Birds all Singing

Something to do with territory makes them sing,
Or so we are told—they woo no sweet and fair,
But tantalise and transfigure the morning air
With coarse description of any other cock bird
That dare intrude a wing
In their half-acre—bumptious and absurd.

Come out and fight, they cry, and roulades of
Tumbling-down sweetness and ascending bliss
Elaborate unrepeatable ancestries;
And impossible deformities still to come
Rise like angels above
The tenement windows of their sylvan slum.

Not passion but possession.   A miserly
Self-enlargement that muddles mine and me
Says the half-acre is the bird, and he,
Deluded to that grandeur, swells, and with
A jolly roundelay
Of boasts and curses establishes a myth.

NORMAN MacCAIG

The human figure underneath the boughs
Takes strictly down, as false as a machine,
The elements of the seen or the half-seen,
And with the miracle of his ear notes all
The singing bird allows,
And feels it innocent, calls it pastoral.

Creations clumsily collide and make
The bird and man more separate.   The man,
Caught up in the lie the bird began,
Feigns a false acre that the world can't hold
Where all is for his sake;
It is the touchstone proving him true gold.

So he, his own enlargement also, thinks
A quiet thought in his corner that creates
Territories of existence, private states
Of being where trespassers are shot at sight;
And myth within myth blinks
Its blind eyes on the casual morning light.

Under or over, nothing truly lies
In its own lucidity.   Creation moves
Restlessly through all its hates or loves
And leaves a wild scenario in its place
Where birds shake savage cries
Like clenched fists in the world's uncaring face.

And man, with straws of singing in his hair,
Strolls in his Bedlam transfiguring every fact,
In full possession of what he never lacked,
The power of being not himself—till with
A twitch of the morning air
Time topples bird and man out of their myth.

INDEX OF FIRST LINES

INDEX OF FIRST LINES

INDEX OF FIRST LINES

INDEX OF FIRST LINES

INDEX OF FIRST LINES

INDEX OF FIRST LINES

INDEX OF FIRST LINES

INDEX OF AUTHORS

INDEX OF AUTHORS